From Berlin

TOPOGRAPHICS

From Berlin

Armando

Translated by
SUSAN MASSOTTY

REAKTION BOOKS

Published by Reaktion Books Ltd
11 Rathbone Place, London W1P 1DE, UK

First published in English 1996

This book consists of extracts from *Uit Berlin,
Machthebbers, Krijgsgewoel* and *We Waren Zo Heerlijk Jong,*
first published in the Dutch language.

English language translation © Susan Massotty, 1996
The publishers would like to acknowledge the financial
support received from the Foundation for the Production
and Translation of Dutch Literature, which has made this
English-language edition possible.

Translated by Susan Massotty
The translator wishes to thank David Alexander
and Alan Broad for their assistance.
Grateful acknowledgement is made to Scott Rollins
for his earlier translation of 'The Nose'.

Designed by Ron Costley
Photoset by Parker Typesetting Service, Leicester
Printed and bound in Great Britain
by The Alden Press, Oxford

British Library Cataloguing in Publication Data

Armando
    From Berlin. – (Topographics)
    1. Travel
    I. Title II. Series
    910.4

ISBN 0 948462 87 6

From Berlin

The House

Some of those surly-looking mansions immediately make me think, hmm, I'd like to see the inside of that one, even though I know it might be a huge disappointment. Most of them have been modernized. What's left from the old days? Nothing, or very little. But *this* house still has everything, everything.

The spry old gentleman who, with a little prodding on my part, showed me the house, from top to bottom, tells me that even the inside doors and wainscoting haven't been repainted. And yet the place doesn't look run-down.

His father had a small publishing business and once said to an architect friend of his: If I ever have enough money, you can build me a house. Twelve years later the time had come; the house was built in 1912. The spry old gentleman of today was then three years old.

The Schlachtensee area of Berlin. The house is surrounded by trees. 'Here,' he says, 'this used to be the living-room. Yes, it is a bit on the large side. I occasionally light a fire, but I rarely ever sit here. To be honest, we almost always sit in the kitchen. And over here in this corner is where we put the Christmas tree.

'Every once in a while I also sit in this room: my father's study, now mine. The bookcase hasn't been changed either. Except that my father had more books than I do. And this is the ladies' sitting-room. Look at the ceiling. Beautiful, eh? What do you think? Beautiful, eh?

'This was the dining-room. Everything is still the same: the enormous table, the chairs, the floor, the wallpaper, everything. Except that we don't eat here anymore. Look at the beautiful workmanship here. These joints, for example. People can't do that anymore these days, not the idiots we have now. Anyway, my father sat in this large chair, and the rest of us were seated according to age. I sat, wait a minute, let me think, I sat here. And my mother sat there, between the two youngest children.

7

'We used to put our birthday gifts on the table in that large alcove. In the morning a curtain was hung in front of the alcove. The birthday boy or girl wasn't the only one to receive presents. There were little gifts for the rest of us children as well, and these were arrayed on that tiled border. Take a good look at those tiles. Oh, when I think about gifts in the old days. What counted wasn't how much it cost, but how useful it was. Each child's needs were taken into careful consideration, and sometimes that meant you received a very inexpensive present. Every once in a while I go to visit friends, and you should see the children's rooms. Sickening, absolutely SICKENING! There are thirty or forty teddy bears. They've got everything their little hearts' could desire, as long as it's expensive. And they're bored out of their minds.

'My own grandchildren are the same. Whenever they're here I invariably find myself yelling: *Schnauze*! In other words, shut up. But one of the little squirts is liable to snap right back: 'bastard' or 'pig' – they're real city kids. They really make me laugh. They're just as cheeky as their grandfather. Me, I mean.

'Here in this corner is where the maid stood. The food was passed to her through this hatch. Architects thought of everything in those days. Look, down by the floorboard, a little rectangle was cut into the wall, to make it easier for the maid to stand there. She could slide her feet into the wall, so to speak. Sometimes I think that modern architects have smaller brains. They can't think anymore. But let's move on and not bother ourselves with the junk in people's heads.

'Unfortunately, our maids were always ugly as sin. That was my mother's doing. No, not because of my father, heavens no, he was far too good. No, because of us boys. So my brothers and I were never initiated into the rites of love or ravished by a maid, unlike the stories we used to hear. No, unfortunately not. I did do other things that weren't allowed. Besides masturbating day and night, I occasionally went to a bar a little further down the lake. The maids and the other servants went there to dance on their days off or whatever. I didn't dare go inside, but stood at

8

the entrance with my nostrils flared, sniffing up all those womanly smells. Female sweat and cheap perfume, an ungodly stench, but I thought it was heavenly. It excited me no end. And then I'd go back home with that awful smell in my nose, in the delightful realization that I'd done something that was forbidden. I didn't talk to anyone about it, but thought of it as my very own personal secret.

'And this is where the servants slept. All the rooms face south and have a balcony. No, they didn't go home at night, not even when their parents lived in Berlin. They were really part of the family. Birthdays, Christmas, they always spent here with us.

'We also had a gardener. He lived with his wife in the gardener's cottage. He spent all day working in the garden. I don't do much gardening now. I'm letting it run wild, I think it's a lot prettier that way. So you see how far the bourgeoisie has sunk. Look, here in the hallway there used to be a cupboard full of electrical equipment. My parents could use it to phone the staff, though they never did. Even then they thought it wasn't progressive. I always say: that cupboard symbolizes the decline of the bourgeoisie. In the old days you could call the servants, and now the cupboard has been nailed shut and covered with modern art.

'I'd like to do up the upstairs and sell it. I have to, I'm up to my neck in debt. Here's where my parents slept, and we six children slept in these three rooms. I shared a room with my brother. In those days it was usual for a young man to go to the city and look for a room in a garret the day before he received his school-leaving certificate. If your landlady was the understanding type, you could take girls there. And study, of course. The last thing you wanted was to hang around your parents' house.

'I'm the only one of the six children who's still alive. One of my brothers was killed in the war. He was a good boy, who never quarrelled with my father. I always did. Actually, I was the only one with any ambition, and I still use my mind, so that keeps you going longer.

9

'My brother was a doctor at Stalingrad when he was young. One of the "heroes of Stalingrad," as Hitler so nicely put it. Right about the time he was killed they discovered that he was a quarter Jewish. We received a letter saying he'd been given a dishonourable discharge from the Wehrmacht, but as luck would have it, he was already dead. That's the way things went in those days.

'I still remember how shocked I once was as a child when our nanny twisted my Stalingrad brother's ear and said, "You little Jewboy." I'd never heard that expression before.

'My father was half-Jewish, which meant during the Nazi era that you weren't allowed to have any servants under the age of forty. At that time friends of theirs were living upstairs, and they supposedly had the servants. But to be on the safe side, my parents had a brick wall built, so that it looked as if there were two houses, if you know what I mean.

'After the war about forty Russians were quartered in this house. My parents were allowed to live in the gardener's cottage. You see, my father had just come back from a concentration camp. The Russians treated my parents with respect. An exception. Then the Americans wanted the house, but my father used his connections and was able to prevent it.

'Now I'm still here. I've had two unsuccessful marriages, all my fault of course, since I'm an absolute scoundrel. Oh, I'm as bad as they come. I raised my six daughters in this house. Or tried to, since raising children isn't exactly my strong point. A couple of them were visiting today with their kids. One of my daughters was a Maoist for a while, but that's gradually wearing off. The woman with the big derrière who was just leaving when you arrived is also one of my daughters. At the moment I'm living together with a young woman who's a real jewel. She's my *Schnupperchen,* my sweetheart. Before you came she told me I should behave myself and that I should also say something nice about her, so now I've done that.

'Would you care for some more wine or would you rather dance a tango. Right then, we'll drink some more wine.'

Remains

Berlin is an ugly city with beautiful remains. Berlin was badly mutilated by bombs, but not destroyed beyond recognition like Dresden or some of the cities in the Ruhr. Afterwards, it was still possible to tell which streets were which. Unlike Dresden, but Erich Kästner has described this in his diary.

What do I mean by beautiful remains? I mean the few lovely buildings, erected decades ago by the bourgeoisie, which have been left undisturbed in dreary cities ruined by post-war architecture. After May 1945 it was necessary to build residential areas fast; people wanted a roof over their heads again. These neighbourhoods are vast spiritual wastelands, yet Berlin is full of them. At a later stage, concrete high-rises popped up everywhere. Utopian architects assured us that they were the ultimate in aesthetic pleasure and that they would make humanity happy, but I, for one, find them depressing.

And yet the war is not the chief offender. After 1945 people demolished countless jaunty little houses and buildings from the late nineteenth century. Here too the rule was: new is good, old is ugly, out with the old. In recent years, people have become more cautious about knocking things down. The frenzy of modernization has abated somewhat. People are back on the right track. They're renovating.

In the meantime, a question has arisen: can you make a sweeping statement of that sort about modern architecture? Can I say that I loathe all (or nearly all) of post-war architecture? No. Because then, what about modern art? What about your own paintings? Exactly.

Berlin is a young city. It doesn't have a majestic medieval past. Oh, here and there you might run across a dilapidated village church looking in disgruntlement at the city around it, but there are no proud Romanesque or Gothic cathedrals. You do see a host of churches built in neo-styles, mostly during the last

11

century, but we won't hold that against them. Better a neo-church than no church. A little circumspection can't hurt.

So Berlin may not be a beautiful city, but it is exciting. What makes it exciting is the occasionally unbearable tension between a seemingly carefree present and an oppressive past. Berlin is a city teeming with places and traces. The traces of a terrifying Reich, frequently overgrown and choked with weeds, are still very much in evidence. For that matter, the many witnesses are still alive, a fact that bears repeating.

Witnesses who kept on believing in that Reich until the very end. Witnesses who went from total infatuation to deep disappointment, mostly because things were going badly. Witnesses who were too young to know better and now look back in astonishment at that period. Witnesses who suffered. And witnesses who simply went about their lives, as best they could, and now conveniently live in the past. Because, as we all know, the past is wonderful, once it's been filtered by time and memory. The worst part is that an alarming number of young people know nothing about the past, and either don't want to know or are unable to find out, and their numbers are growing.

A great many of the witnesses who are still alive can do little more these days than shuffle listlessly from room to room. But back then they were young and gay, since they had enough to keep them busy and the world belonged to them, or so they thought.

These witnesses never cease to interest me. That's why I like to go wherever older people gather together. All those mysterious conversations going on around me. This titbit of information, that morsel of knowledge. A great deal, far too much, will never come to my ears. I overhear a few snatches of their conversations: 'in the war . . .', and then their voices fade away again. Do they do that on purpose? Of course not.

But I can't question everyone!

Such as on a melancholy afternoon in a German *Kaffeehaus*. I see the pianist and the violinist chatting with the waiter: three elderly gentlemen. The violinist briefly rests his hand on the

12

waiter's shoulder. Old army pals? What were these three men to each other and where were they? I can't question everyone! Perish the thought. And yet I want to go on, as long as I can, recording their experiences, or at any rate the bits which have stuck in their memories. I haven't yet talked to *all* Berliners over the age of seventy.

Or should I get up in the middle of a bierfest, a concert in the Philharmonic or a jolly senior-citizens get-together and ask everyone who was, well, who was anybody during the war to stand up and tell me what they were and where they were doing it. I can't do that, however much I'd like to. Ignorance, though, is bliss. Let well enough alone!

But the past is always lying in ambush for me. It rears its ugly head in the simplest of conversations.

'So, do you like it in Berlin?'

Yes, I do. A lot.

'Where do you live, if you don't mind my asking?'

In Frohnau. (That's where I lived at the time.)

'Hmm, right up in the north of the city, near the Wall. Hmm. Do you ever go near there, near the Wall?'

Yes, I do. Every day, actually. (It marked the spot where the residential neighbourhood with the tree-lined streets and quiet houses ended and the countryside began. There, where the two had always met, was the Wall. In this part of Berlin you could look through the Wall, since it consisted of a heavy, sturdy kind of chicken wire. Behind it there was a field which had lain fallow for years, a wasteland. With watchtowers and searchlights. I used to go past it every day with my dog, and every day several pairs of arms would be raised inside the watchtowers as the guards eyed us through their binoculars. Hello, stranger.)

'Listen,' the man continued, 'at the border, where that wasteland begins, there used to be a camp. Did you know that?'

What's that. What's he saying?

'Yes, there used to be a camp. Not a concentration camp, but a camp for foreign workers who volunteered or were forced to work in factories in Berlin. There were also Dutch workers.'

13

Oh, that. So that's where the barracks used to be. There isn't a single trace left.

'And after the capitulation,' the man rattled on, 'the foreign workers all went back home. Most of them, including the Dutch, travelled on foot. They all behaved themselves. Except for the Poles, who went around looting and raping. But the others, as I said, all behaved themselves. And after that the barracks were knocked down.'

Much later. 'Where do you live, if I may be so bold as to ask?'

I live on Bundesallee.

'Where on Bundesallee, if you don't mind my asking? It's such a long street.'

Between Friedrich Wilhelm Platz and Walther Schreiber Platz. In Friedenau.

'Oh, there. Then you must live near that big factory. Isn't that right? It used to be operated by the Luftwaffe during the war. They made precision instruments, you know. Is it still there?'

Yes, it's still there. Although nowadays they're manufacturing something else.

The lucky few who are already familiar with my work and my motifs will realize that I'm now in the lion's den. Oddly enough, I find it reassuring. It gives me a feeling of finally being *home* in the uncomfortable past. But of course it occasionally gets on my nerves.

After all, the task I've set for myself in Berlin is to study 'the enemy', to observe the enemy. The Germans themselves have a nice word for it: *Feindbeobachtung*. A series of large canvases which I've painted here have been entitled *Feindbeobachtung* because, though it gives me little pleasure to say so, that's what I'm doing here in Berlin. But don't I observe the enemy in other places as well? Isn't that what I'm always doing? That's a good question. And the answer may be a long time in coming.

Fragments

MAN: Before 1933 I had more fun with ten marks than today's youth with a hundred or more. Everywhere you went, in all the cafés, there were small dance bands, sometimes consisting of no more than three musicians, and each of them could play several instruments. Oh, I can't begin to tell you how much fun that was! It's such a pity, but there's no one you can talk to about these kinds of things. No one! Oh, I sometimes bring it up with older people, but young people aren't interested. They only listen to American music. Not German, but American music. There's a station here, the AFN, and they have it on all day long. Nothing but American music. They think it's wonderful. Oh, there's no point in talking about it.

*

WOMAN to her dog (corner of Welfenallee and Kammgasse): Look, Baby, here's where Mummy fell down the other day. You remember, don't you?

*

MAN: In recent years I've met quite a few emigrés. I mean the people who left Germany in the Thirties and haven't been back since. You can hardly believe the way they talk. Their German is rather old-fashioned. It's beautiful and colourful, with words – especially adjectives – we haven't used in years. Our language has undergone enormous changes. Mostly owing to the influence of television. I think of it as a plague.

*

WOMAN: You know who managed to come home from the war? The rowdies and the drunks. They're the ones who came back. Most of the women in my neighbourhood still say: If only mine had been killed. But no, they came back.

*

MAN: I was also in a concentration camp. In Dachau. Yes, I was, but then *after* the war. As a POW. And we had a much tougher time of it there than they did during the war, I can tell you that.

*

MAN: You bet! Of course I supported National Socialism. You bet I did. I came from a family of eight: father, mother and six boys. All unemployed. Then Hitler came along, and first my father got a job and then all my brothers. I was the only one to volunteer for the army, because they said you'd be eligible for a civil service job after the war. Well, I wound up in the Navy, and was captured the first time I went into action, so I spent the rest of the war in a POW camp in England. I had the time of my life in that camp. You won't catch *me* complaining about it. My mates called me The Baron, because I had such a bloody great moustache. The British thought I really was a baron, and they spoiled me rotten. Food, drink, even women. That's the gospel truth. So you see, I had the time of my life. And now I'm a taxi driver. I earn a good living, and otherwise, if we'd won, I'd have been a postman or something. God, even the thought of it makes me shudder.

*

WOMAN: Hitler was a bad person. Even as a child. He used to climb trees and rob birds' nests. That means he was destructive even as a child. His parents were ashamed of him, his brother never wanted to talk to him again. He was a bad person. Besides that, he wasn't even German. It's his fault that my husband was killed. He *had to* die, Hitler wanted all the men to die. Whether they wanted to or not. And then what he did to the Jews. Terrible. You just don't *do* that kind of thing.

*

MAN: If you think the lads who were in an elite corps like the U-boat crews or the Paratroopers or the Waffen SS were real Nazis, you're making a big mistake. Don't make me laugh. Listen, I was a little older when I had to join up. All I wanted was to get out of it alive, and because I was a quarter Jewish, I was also hoping to gum up the works for the Nazis wherever I could. But those kids, young, healthy and strong, the types we referred to as *richtige Kerle*, real men, wanted to be in the units where something was going on, where there was a little action. Take the blokes in those fighter planes – they were only interested in banging away at the enemy. They thought it was fun. You had the same types on the other side. Those boys weren't real Nazis, 'course not. After the war they got in touch with their enemies. They met, and sat around talking as if they'd just finished a game. They're still doing it. It's like one of those jousts during the Middle Ages. It has nothing to do with Nazis.

Trudel

You want to know something terrible? At the flea-market in Berlin you can buy bundles of letters.

Letters.

I haven't done it yet. For a variety of reasons. First, you have to buy the entire bundle. That's not easy. You can't stand there reading every letter one by one. You just can't, the vendor doesn't like it. Still, I thumbed through a couple and noticed they weren't arranged by person. So if you buy a pile, there's a big chance it won't be complete, and you'll never be able to find out how it all ends. There are even letters written by soldiers, in which case you'd be dying to know what happened to the poor guys. Just the thought of getting a partial exchange of letters is enough to discourage me. It'd be one more thing to worry about.

Second, it's none of my business. Or rather, I have a vague feeling it isn't. So I still haven't bought any. I often stand there leafing through them and hesitating, but in the end I don't buy them. I surprise myself sometimes.

Every so often I do buy photograph albums. Snapshots. Not the ones made after 1950. That's not so far away, that's just within my reach. It's the time before that that keeps slipping from my grasp. Just when I think I've got hold of it, someone or something yanks it out of my hand, and that hurts. Yes, it's a constant struggle.

The albums are really quite touching, because they're visible traces that might, just might, tell a story or evoke something, though they tend to conceal more than they reveal.

I have one of them, put together by the husband with tender care. Sometimes he arranged the snapshots in daring groups and added mischievous comments. He glued dried flowers around their wedding picture. And in the front of the album he wrote 'My dearest Trudel 1906' and surrounded it with a meticulously drawn curlicue.

A childless couple who enjoyed themselves. That much you can deduce from the album. He's a university graduate, has a good job and walks through the park every day on his way home. During World War I a soldier comes to stay, a relative who's in the service. They play tennis, go on modest little outings and furnish their home, as one was supposed to, with impeccable taste. He takes a picture of their street from the balcony. All the rest fades away, dissolves into nothingness, retreats into the background.

An address has been written next to the picture of their street. So I check it out. With butterflies in my stomach, for some odd reason, I turn into the street and look for the house. Yes, I'm in luck, the house is still there, the street is still there. Okay, I'm here. Now what? Nothing. What am I going to see? What I already know: that it's not the way it used to be. That it's inhabited by a number of contemporary beings, and while they're undoubtedly much more emancipated than the previous occupants, the discontent is clearly visible on their faces. But this is no way to view the surreptitious panting of time.

The man who lives there now was lying under an old car, tinkering with the engine, a radio at his side. His wife, standing on the pavement next to their little girl, informed him that he was an arsehole and gave the child an angry shove. To my astonishment, the child laughed. The mother glanced at her in surprise out of the corner of her eye and calmed down.

No, the husband and wife in the photo album are gone. Their life has been reduced to a few snapshots in a flea-market, and one day a grumpy man comes along and buys up the rest of their life, even haggling over the price, since that's what you're supposed to do, and yes, the longer it goes on, the cheaper the life of this couple gets. Is this why the husband and wife went to all that trouble? Yes.

In my opinion, time behaves outrageously. I'd like to call a halt to the whole business for a while. Lay it down on the table, oh, do be careful, put a lamp beside it, and take a leisurely look. Well, you can forget that.

The past? The past is a patch of darkness. It's black with a zillion shades of grey. The future is white. Feel free to scribble on it to your heart's content.

As the story goes, three men descended into the realm of darkness. One went mad, the second blind. The third returned safe and sound and said he'd found himself. That could hardly have been a barrel of fun.

Places

If I leave my house and turn left, I first come to a small bookshop. If I ask the four or five elderly ladies who work there (I still haven't worked out their exact number) about a book, they start running around like a lot of headless chickens. They exclaim and shout questions back and forth, rummage through drawers and cupboards, search high and low and generally get in each other's way. All four or five of them. Sorry, but we just can't find it, what are we going to do. Would you mind ordering the book for me – again. Of course not, oh where's the order book, what happened to the order book, do you know where the order book is, oh, now I can't find the pen. How this is going to end is anybody's guess.

A few yards down the street, on the corner, is a house which, until recently, was being renovated. A house like any other. Nothing strange about that. But if you're the type who reads everything you can get your hands on and takes notes, you'll realize that this ordinary building just happens to be the house from which the *Rote Kapelle* transmitted during the war. I take this opportunity to bid farewell to those who have never heard of this resistance group before.

A house like this is a *place*. Month after month you walk by it, a nice house, mind you, and suddenly it's a place. What a shame. How magnificent.

Somewhere else in Berlin, there's a huge mound of sand. Okay, so what's the story behind that huge mound of sand. Nothing much – except that once upon a time it used to be the headquarters of the Gestapo, that's all. Until recently, the Wall ran right by it. A bit further away there's a building, now standing with its eyes closed, that once belonged to the Nazis: the ruins of the Reich Air Ministry. Just imagine, people used to go in and out of the Gestapo building, officials and otherwise. In all likelihood they were just ordinary people.

Berlin is a carefree city that stays put.

Look, over there, that weed-filled, rubbish-strewn site was once the location of the beautiful *Volksgerichtshof*, People's Court, where the Nazi judge Roland Friesler used to bully the defendants and condemn them to death with great glee. During one of the air raids towards the end of the war, a beam fell right on top of him. Dead as a doornail. Justice triumphs. Investigators have discovered that before 1933 he was an ardent Communist. I don't remember where. Kassel, I think, but I don't have my fiendish-fact-files at my fingertips.

And this is the hotel where Giorgi Dimitroff and his cronies were arrested for supposedly having set fire to the Reichstag on 27 February 1933. The trial took place in Leipzig. After the war, the East Germans reconstructed the entire courtroom scene and put it on display. The judges sat here, the hero Dimitroff sat there, fat Goering ranted and raved on this spot here, and so-and-so sat over there. The Dutch pyromaniac, Marinus van der Lubbe, was given short shrift. Since he wasn't actually a card-carrying Communist, he was depicted as a muddleheaded nobody. Unimportant.

Back to Berlin. A city full of blind walls. I can't even begin to tell you how beautiful those blind walls are.

Over here is Potsdamer Platz, once one of the busiest squares in Europe. Until a few years ago, weed-ridden tramlines continued under the Wall and ended abruptly thirty feet away. If you looked over the Wall, you could see what was left of Potsdamer Platz: an empty field, barbed wire and rabbits. As for that hump to the left, well, that was Hitler's bunker. The Reich Chancellery was also located there.

Berlin is a city full of snares. You imagine.

This silent street. On one side, a railway line runs along a recessed road. On the other side, next to a few allotment gardens, there are a couple of old brick buildings with pseudo-Baroque facades. Used to be army barracks. It's now a firm of builders.

The basement of this building served as a forerunner of the

German concentration camps. After the Reichstag fire, the political opponents of the Stormtroopers were tortured and beaten here. In the basement. If you want, you can peer through the windows. Or you can walk past and pretend you know nothing, act as if nothing's the matter. As if it were any old building, and not a place.

And these streets, Friedrichstrasse and Wilhelmstrasse. Yes, these streets. I can't begin to tell you everything that went on here. 'Oh, they used to be delightful streets. There were bands playing everywhere, or sometimes just a harmonica. And nice shops. Oh, they were so delightful.'

A few years ago I was given an odd book: *Berlin in a Death Struggle 1945: French SS Volunteers as the Last Defenders of the Reich Chancellery*. The writer, Jean Mabire, is a Frenchman. He's a great admirer of the volunteers. The book is therefore 'suspect', the kind you're not supposed to read. So who reads books like these? I do. I want to learn a little something about my vociferous fellow human beings.

And what did I find? That Berlin, the capital of the Third Reich, was defended, up to the last minute, by a handful of fanatical French volunteers: three hundred men. Norwegians, Danes and Dutch were allowed to join in as well, but for the most part they were French. The volunteers, the majority of whom were very young, were surprised to see sizeable numbers of German officers and soldiers sprawling apathetically in cellars and bunkers, awaiting the inevitable approach of the enemy. They wanted to make it home alive.

The French didn't. They fought for every house, for every room. Right there in Friedrichstrasse and Wilhelmstrasse. French volunteers who had sworn a solemn oath: loyal and courageous to the end.

One of history's quirks, and few Berliners even know of it.

Fortunately, the author had spoken to some of the former volunteers. In his book, he tells us how they're getting along. Thirty of them survived the final weeks of the war and were then roughly forty years older. One of them, who was missing an eye, had become a Benedictine monk. He said he prayed a lot for the men at whose side he fought.

And this square was where the huge book-burning rally took place on 10 May 1933. Carl von Ossietzky worked in this house, and there, in that quiet street, is where Stauffenberg lived, and this mysterious-looking mansion, the one with the pillars, is where the Wannsee Conference was held. A villa with a lovely view of the Wannsee.

I know many, many more defenceless places and other things of that nature. But why should I list them all. Before you know it, I will have become an unpaid but miserable guide.

It's odd, living in a city full of people and walls that are pockmarked with bullet holes.

Fragments

WOMAN: My father was a botanist. He was what you call an absent-minded professor. He didn't even recognize his own children when he saw them in the street. And he was forever wearing socks or shoes that didn't match. We'd have to chase after him on our bicycles: Father, here's the right sock. He walked around like a pauper, in an old pair of trousers, and a worn-out jacket with holes. I hated that when I was a girl. But during the war he became an officer, and he was transformed into a totally different person. His uniform was always impeccable. Absolutely impeccable! And woe betide any one of his soldiers whose uniform wasn't in order. An odd kind of schizophrenia. And yet he remained an anti-Nazi through it all. He helped people where he could – I heard that later from some of his colleagues. He refused to make concessions, but there was that strange militarism. He had such a strong sense of duty! He was discharged from the army in '44. I still think that was because he didn't smoke or drink. Actually, he was a real misfit.

*

WOMAN: Yes, I was here in Berlin during all the air raids. I was alone with my four children. We spent weeks in the basement. On the very first night I realized I was going to have to take care of myself, that nobody was going to help me and my four children. So I said to myself, Elisabeth, now's the time to show what you're made of. From that moment on, I was always very calm. Somehow, I seemed to radiate calmness. Even soldiers who were on leave wanted to sit near me in the shelter. When we're at the front, they said, we've got a job to do, but here, during an air raid, all you can do is wait. That made them nervous, and sitting next to me seemed to calm them down. Funny, isn't it? Once in a while, my children used to ask me: Mama, aren't you scared? No, I'd say, I'm not scared. But I was. I don't mind admitting that from time to time I even said a prayer or two.

*

WOMAN: We were really lucky, only one member of my family was killed. Just one. A cousin of mine. He froze to death in Russia that first winter. After all, they hadn't been issued any winter clothes. Froze to death, poor boy.

*

MAN: After the capitulation I wandered around Bavaria for a while; I'd managed to get hold of civilian clothes. Then I spent a month or two supposedly as an interpreter for the Americans. Gee, was I ever impressed by those guys! They were so nonchalant. It took me weeks to figure out who the officer in charge of our group was. That kind of thing was inconceivable in Germany. Their job was to round up any stray German soldiers who were roaming the countryside. So we drove around the back roads, but seeing as how those guys were too lazy to walk even a couple of yards, I got out and combed the bushes from time to time. And if I came across a fellow soldier, I said to him, listen, the Amis are looking for you, and he retreated farther into the bushes. We didn't pick up a single German soldier, but we sure had a lot of fun.

*

WOMAN: During the war my brother-in-law was what was known as a 'hundred and fifty percenter'. A fervent Nazi, in other words. He worked for a large company, and whenever we said to him, why don't you go down and enlist if you believe in it so much, he'd reply, oh, but my company can't possibly do without me. One night my brother and I went to see him. My brother was on leave, and he told us what he'd been through in Russia and began talking about what was being done to Russian civilians and Jews, until my brother-in-law banged his fist on the table and shouted: I forbid you to talk like that about the Führer and the soldiers of the Third Reich in my house. So my brother said: I believe it's time for us to leave. We never saw my brother-in-law again. Towards the end of the war, he was living in a village east of Berlin. But when the Russians came, it wasn't safe there either. He was afraid the villagers would turn him in. So he poisoned his two children, two darling little girls, shot his wife and then shot himself, and believe me, that was the best thing he'd ever done in his life. But the worst part was that his wife was still alive. She woke up and saw her husband and her two children lying dead beside her. She had a bullet in her head, but she was still alive. After the war, she was operated on twelve times. It was a struggle, but she did her best, she even went to university. Still, about ten years ago she died as a result of the wound. It started to fester or something.

*

WOMAN: I don't remember a thing about the war. While the war was going on, I firmly resolved to forget all that happened, and oddly enough I really don't remember. Ask my husband. I don't remember a thing. I've forgotten it all. Strange.

Her husband: 'Yes, it's absolutely true. She doesn't remember a thing. I do.'

Ladies and Animals

Strange things are going on at the Berlin Zoo. In the aquarium, a noticeable number of fish are swimming around with disgruntled looks, as if a strike is brewing. Elsewhere in the zoo an ape grabs his underlip, pulls it out as far as he can, and looks at it for a long, long time. Another large ape wearily descends a few steps of his jungle gym and picks up a pebble. He climbs back up and throws the pebble into the crowd with a gesture of boredom. And what about the carelessly draped nest of snakes. What should we make of that? Or of the hippopotamuses, one of whom is called Würstchen and the other Plumps. What should we make of all that, and what should we do?

So, to my regret, the meaning of creation also remains exceedingly unclear to me here in the Berlin Zoo. But fortunately, most visitors view this peculiar animal business in a more lighthearted frame of mind. They take a quick look at some beast, say 'Wow, that one's really super', and stroll on.

A goodly portion of the spectators consist of older women. Their husbands were killed during the war or have simply passed away, their children and grandchildren have no time for them, and young people never, ever, offer them a seat in the tram or bus. So they turn to the animals with total dedication.

A black ape, a gorilla, leans against the glass wall of his cage and stares dejectedly into space. An elderly lady arrives. 'Oh,' she exclaims, 'you look a lot better than yesterday!'

The ape rallies. The woman claps her hands, without making a sound. The ape cautiously imitates her, with his fingertips barely touching. Next she shows him the contents of her bag. ('Look, a packet of cigarettes, lipstick, a handkerchief. Take a good look.') The ape does seem to look. The woman then places the palms of her hands against the glass, and the ape places his large hands against hers.

'Bye bye, see you tomorrow,' the woman says and disappears

from sight. Other visitors imitate her, likewise place their hands against the glass, but the ape takes no notice. Instead, he plays with his faeces.

Another gorilla, Knorke, an unfriendly type, is giving the female gorillas Gigi and Cocotte a bad time. He stalks around them menacingly, and every once in a while he hauls off and belts them. Knorke is clearly a pain in the neck, and the little old ladies make an attempt to call him to order. They do this with full understanding of the male of the species. Men, they know from experience, are difficult creatures, but necessary none the less. So instead of calling Knorke names, they exclaim, 'Be careful, Knorke. Watch out, Gigi, look behind you. Oh, Knorke, why are you such a crosspatch today? Don't hit her, Knorke. Be nice.'

Knorke peers at the chorus of women and, yes, he does quieten down. 'Well done,' the ladies say, 'good boy.'

In the meantime Gigi, who's dangling from a beam, produces a large, yellow turd, which falls to the ground. Without a trace of laughter, the little old ladies imitate the sound of the falling turd. 'Plop!' they exclaim. In this connection, and yet an aside: gorillas are vegetarians.

Another darling of the ladies is a large elephant seal named Bolle. He tries to stay under water for long periods of time. The ladies call in their faint voices: 'Bolle, come on out!' At last the leviathan rises snorting to the surface and hangs over the edge of the pool. The ladies carry on a lengthy discussion with him or loudly imitate his snorts.

A few days later it seems that something's the matter. Bolle doesn't feel like eating his herring. The keeper walks away shaking his head. Bolle hangs over the tank for a noticeably long time and snorts through one nostril. He has large, brown eyes and looks quite lovable. But here too appearances are deceptive: seals are not very tolerant of each other. Younger seals who swim too close are immediately given a warning slap, but then that makes some sense.

'Bolle, you're a real lazybones,' yells a man with his daughter on his shoulders.

'How can you say such a thing?' exclaims a little old lady. 'Bolle isn't lazy. How can you say such a thing? Bolle is old, he's twelve. And besides that, he's not well.'

'Bollechen!' calls another lady, and her voice breaks. 'Bollechen, *bitte*!'

'Yes, he's ill,' the lady continues. 'He hasn't eaten for four days. Oh, if only he doesn't die, our Bolle.'

The next day, I read in the morning paper that Bolle had died of some intestinal disorder. In a lengthy obituary, the newspaper outlined Bolle's praiseworthy life. It made me sad, since he had such nice eyes.

A few weeks ago a new miracle occurred. Two cuddly brutes took up residence in the Berlin Zoo: two pandas (*Ailuropoda melanoleuca*). The male is called Bao Bao (*Schätzchen* in German), and the female Tian Tian (*Himmelchen* in German). A gift to Germany from China.

What are pandas? Pandas are enchanting creatures with ears. That much is clear, but it's hardly enough. The giant panda, threatened with extinction, lives in the wild solely in the rain forests of southwest China. Biologists believe that there are fewer than a thousand pandas left. That's all. What a pity.

Pandas don't like noise, they sleep a lot, they're loners, and they eat sitting up, mostly bamboo. Because bamboo has so few calories, they have to eat lots of it, and I mean lots: nine pounds a day. Besides that, every morning and evening they get half a gallon of mash, consisting of rice, corn, soya beans, vegetables, sugar, salt, eggs and vitamins. Well, they seem to like it.

What about the love life of the panda? Pandas have an alarmingly infrequent love life. They either don't replace themselves at all, or just barely. They're lazy. They're chaste.

Recently, after a series of time-consuming diplomatic negotiations, a female panda from London was taken to a male panda in Moscow. For weeks, the male behaved like a bashful schoolboy. Then he suddenly got the urge and made his move. The female immediately punched him on the nose. After two months she was returned to London. She travelled first class. In addition to bamboo, she ate milk chocolate of the highest quality. She gave the impression of being satisfied.

I've now come to view the two Berlin pandas. They're asleep. It's true, they're very appealing. I can't help but wonder who designed such nice-looking creatures, and am unable to suppress a silly grin.

And there they are again, the little old ladies, with their noses pressed to the glass. They don't know each other, but they're chatting away, as if they were lifelong friends. They wait. They wait for hours until one of the sleeping pandas moves. He stretches and looks at the crowd through his black eyepatches. Then something strange happens.

The women call out 'Ooooohh!' in their high voices, and they all begin to wave. But the panda merely shifts his position and goes back to sleep, with his arm once again over his face. The women continue to wait for the next sign of life. For hours. Their faces, hardened by life's trials and tribulations, relax and take on an expression of love, you might even say devotion. Women can be so beautiful, but that's a known fact.

They don't talk *about* the pandas, but *to* the pandas. They don't say 'Oh, isn't he sweet' or 'Isn't he lazy,' but 'Oh, *you're* so sweet' or '*You're* so lazy.' The other ladies agree. They speak informally to the bears, addressing them as *du* rather than *Sie*. And that's good.

A young Asian comes to have a look. 'Oh, look,' says one of the ladies, 'a compatriot of theirs.' The young man gently taps the glass to attract the attention of the two animals. The ladies put their heads together and whisper, 'Ah, he's seeking contact. Isn't that nice?'

The pandas sleep. The ladies wait. 'Oh, if only we could pet them for a moment.'

'Do you think they'd be soft?' one of them inquires bashfully.

'Oh,' another exclaims, 'incredibly soft!'

I get talking with one of the keepers. 'Sheer loneliness, my friend,' he says, 'sheer loneliness. The women spend all day here, especially during the summer. They develop a strong

31

attachment to the animals. Have you seen them waving to the pandas? In the old days they used to wave at Hitler the same way.'

I ask him what he did during the war, since he's the right age.

'I didn't wave,' he says, 'but I marched for Hitler, and that was a lot more stupid.'

The German Salute

A black man and a black woman, both between thirty and forty years old, are travelling on the U-Bahn. They're talking merrily away, speaking English.

At the next station, a scrawny German in his late sixties boards the train. He's had a few too many. He sits down on the empty seat across from the two blacks. He stares at them for a while and then asks in English, 'Where are you from?'

The black man looks surprised: '*Bitte*?'

The man repeats, 'Which country are you from?'

The black man answers, '*Aus Berlin. Ich bin Berliner.*'

'No,' the man says. 'No, I'm a Berliner, I live in Berlin.'

'Me too,' the black man says. 'I've lived in Berlin for a long time. I'm a Berliner.'

'No, you're not. You can't be.'

'But I am,' the black man replies. 'I'm a Berliner.'

The German give him a long, hard look, and then stares at the woman. He asks in English, 'Is this your wife?'

'*Bitte?*'

'Is this your wife?'

'*Nein, das is meine Schwester.*'

The man is silent for a moment and then says, 'You're a good boy.'

'*Danke,*' the black man smiles. '*Danke schön.*'

The drunk decides to get off. He shakes the black man's hand a long time, totters towards the door and stands on the platform with his big head pressed against the window, staring at the black man, who nods and grins slightly. The train slowly begins to move, and the drunk suddenly makes the Hitler salute, right in front of the window.

Without a moment's hesitation, the black man returns the salute.

And along with him four other men born during or after the

war, who'd no doubt been eavesdropping, though they hadn't let on. One even puts down his newspaper so he can raise his arm.

So five men inside the train and one man outside are making the Hitler salute. But the men inside are doing it with a weary smile, the way you humour a child by imitating its gesture.

I relate this curious incident to a good friend of mine, the eighty-five-year-old Kurt F.

'Ah, yes,' he says, 'the so-called German salute. That's what we called the Hitler salute, you know the one with the arm stretched out in front. There were people during the Nazi era who simply continued to say "good morning," without sticking their arms out. But on certain occasions, for example when you had to go to one of those Government offices filled with Nazis, that was suspect. I owned a big chemist's, and sometimes I thought it was necessary to make the Hitler salute there, but I compromised by saying "good morning" instead of "Heil Hitler".

'After the war a lot of people couldn't break the habit. They'd start to make the movement, but then they'd pull their arms back when they were half way. It looked pretty comical! Half an arm being raised.

'It happened to me too. Soon after Berlin was captured, my first wife was having a baby in a clinic in the Dahlem district of Berlin. I was there with her, and suddenly the Russians were standing at the door, wanting watches and women.

'And then a strange thing happened. As the Russians came through the door, a lot of the women made the Hitler salute, out of fear. It was very odd. A bunch of women standing around with their arms in the air. Out of fear.

'The Russians were blind drunk. Von Ribbentrop's villa was just across from the clinic, and they'd discovered the wine cellar. I was able to hide my wife in a cupboard, along with a couple of other women. The Russians were very jovial when they saw me. "Comrade," they shouted, and insisted I drink an enormous glass of vodka with them. I said I wasn't allowed to drink because I had a bleeding ulcer, which was why I hadn't been called up, but they wouldn't take no for an answer. They put a gun to my head, so of course I drained the glass. All the women were raped. Regardless of whether they were pregnant or had just given birth, they all got raped in the end. I feel obliged to add, in all honesty, that not all the Russians were like that. Some of them tried to stop their comrades. But I saw one of the drunken soldiers put a machine-gun to the chest of a guy who protested. One of their own comrades!

'Victory had gone to their heads. That's the only explanation I can think of. But, as we say to each other, we survived.'

Fragments

WOMAN: The Nazis had an organization known as *Kraft durch Freude* (Strength through Joy), which organized holidays and that kind of thing for ordinary people like us. That was a real treat. I learned to ride a bicycle in *Kraft durch Freude*. Oh, it was wonderful, I loved zooming along on a bike. I can't do it anymore. I can hardly walk, I'm eighty-six, you know! Oh, if only I could still cycle. *Kraft durch Freude* taught me how. My parents didn't have enough money for things like that.

*

MAN: I was in a Russian POW camp in Siberia until the late 1950s. Compared to others, we weren't so badly off. We lived off tinned goods from the States the entire time. You should have seen how much American aid was pouring into Russia! Of course we were hungry, but the people living near the camp were even hungrier. They came to us to beg for bread. My god, what a primitive country. The Russians are being taken to the cleaners, just like we were back then.

*

MAN: I was stationed in Holland during the war. Towards the end. Twice that I remember, a Dutch person really put me in my place. We were retreating, and we'd been on the road a long time. We'd slept in the street, and I felt dirty. So I rang somebody's doorbell to ask if I could wash my hands and face. No, said the woman, go and knock at number 9, they're crazy about Germans. But ma'am, I said, I'm only asking for a little water, I'm not here as your enemy. To which the woman again replied: Ask at number 9, they're crazy about you people. Of course she meant they were collaborators. Actually, I admired her for saying that, and I didn't go to number 9.

And then there was a shop I always went to. I stopped there to pick up something just as we were leaving, but I had my rifle with me. Would you please leave your rifle outside, said the woman. No, ma'am, I said, I can't do that. We soldiers have to have our rifles with us at all times. You risk severe punishment if you don't. Well then, said the woman, come back after the war without your rifle. I must confess that I went out of that shop with my head hanging. Yes, I did go back after the war, and we shook hands.

*

WOMAN: An older friend of ours has also led a strange life. He was fourteen when the war was over, and full of Nazi ideals. A fanatical member of the Hitler Youth. When the Americans entered his town, you know what he did? He took to his bed and didn't come out of it for six years. *Six years!* His entire world had collapsed. Now he's a businessman, but there's still something strange about him. He collects modern art. That's why we like him so much.

*

MAN: During the last few months of the war I was an officer in France. We were pulling out. We drove and drove, for days at a time, in open trucks. I still remember coming to one of those typically French provincial hotels and scraping the dust out of the grooves in my face with a knife. As you can imagine, I slept like a log that night. The next morning I heard a knock at the door. The man from the hotel, telling me I might want to take a look outside. I looked outside, and the village square was full of American tanks. *Merde!* What do we do now, I asked the man. Well, he said, if you go out the back door, you can cross over the river and then head for Germany. And that's exactly what we did. Oh, no, he wasn't a collaborator or anything. No, the French were just nice people. That's all there is to it.

*

WOMAN: We spent the last days of the war in our bunker, a nice little bunker in our back garden. The whole family was crammed inside. At the time we were living in a tiny little house in a working-class neighbourhood on the outskirts of Berlin, in Köpenick. We were expecting the Russians any minute. Suddenly the door of the bunker flew open and there was a Russian. My father sprang to his feet, stuck out his arm and shouted *Heil Hitler!* What an idiot, eh? Ha ha ha ha. Later we laughed ourselves sick. Not then, but later. Ha ha ha hee hee hee. And the best part is that my father was a Communist from the word go. Hee hee hee. It still makes me laugh, hee hee hee, I can't stop, oh . . . ha ha ha, how embarrassing, an old woman like me, ha ha hee hee hee. No, as it turned out the Russian didn't say anything, but oh . . . ha ha hee hee hee.

Night

I sometimes wonder what I'm doing here in Berlin. Why I don't go live in a cave or a grotto, with friendly animals who fetch my food for me. But no, here I am, in the middle of the night: artists may devote their lives to beauty, but they pay a high price. So now you know, they pay a high price.

I walk as though I'm listening. Do you have any idea of what's been hidden away or concealed here? You won't discover a single trace, of course, but what counts is the fact that you make the *attempt*. What counts is finding a form in which to make the attempt: giving form to the attempt, giving form to your inability to do so.

Wait, something's going on. 'My god,' I hear behind me. 'My god, what's the matter, don't you have your bloody watch on?'

I turn around and see a drunk staring at his empty wrist. An aging Sir Galahad, talking to himself. Bad dreams about long-ago battles. According to my friend Hölderlin, 'God is a person when you're dreaming, a beggar when you're thinking.'

While I plan a series of paintings I intend to call *Wiederkehr* – Return – he starts to mutter. A litany of complaints. About having to sleep on the street in winter clothes in the middle of summer. And the reverse, don't forget the reverse. Plus the occasional freak. Not to mention the thousands of corpses in the garden, dead beetles. From time to time, you can still hear the high-pitched whine of the war. Everything smelled back in those days. The road we officers took. Not a scratch. Venomous cobblestones. A hell of a lot of noise. And everyone watching. They were cheering!

'What were you supposed to do?'

I walk as though I'm listening. The sound of a fist-fight. The smell of a fighting fist.

'You should really listen to me for once.' As I said, I'm listening.

There's a thundershower. 'Which do you prefer?' he asks. 'No, which do you think sounds more *homely*: thunder or ack-ack guns?' Give me ack-ack guns any day. I find them more reassuring. Thunder is a natural phenomenon, an ack-ack gun is a human phenomenon. A man-made product. Something created by people.

I wonder whether you can only survive with a bitter laugh. Sir Galahad keeps asking me questions. Dubious conversations, under the motto, 'A joke a day keeps the doctor away.' Pure desperation. Because people are wretched creatures, mournful scoundrels. Conceited to the bone, with dusty feet.

I stare at the man for a long time. What am I doing – trying to see him as he used to be? I'll never be able to manage that, so I might as well stop trying. All that capsizing of time, isn't it ever going to stop? You act as if time is on your side. You fight against the inevitable. But what else can I do in this city, except try to think about the secrets of others, secrets which happen to blow my way. Who knows, maybe death is being blown along with them. You try to make yourself a master of disguise. But why? Why?

Oh, the artist and his *Wiederkehr* series. He spends too much time in caverns of his own making, lighting the way with a feeble candle that's no match for the merciless draughts. Now and again he sets off on a quest, and that's not exactly fun. Oh, forgive this fool when, in his desperation, he looks around to see if he has any allies. Might there be someone in the distance who nods in agreement and wants to follow? Perhaps. A lone individual or two.

Every once in a while he comes back to mingle with the crowd of onlookers. He talks and laughs, behaves himself occasionally, and hears the numerous reproaches: you shouldn't do this, you ought to do that differently, you've still got a lot to learn. He nods, but his thoughts are elsewhere, and he can't do a thing about it. An inflated ego? Self-glorification? Yes. It happens before the artist's fellow human beings have had a chance to grab him by the legs, pull him down to earth and make him one of them. Stay here. Come down. What's the meaning of this pitiful spectacle?

It's still night. Under a hulking street lamp, a group of God-fearing people are talking and singing about Jesus. Singing. Women with pursed lips, but frivolous footwear. A man is playing the harmonica and they're happy, since they're proselytizing. Who's listening? The alcoholics who hang around the Zoo train station. But what's that? Someone starts to dance, a tall woman with a damp, red face. Watch out, licentious dancing is not on the agenda, licentious dancing is definitely not allowed. An intoxicated woman is dancing on someone's grave.

All of a sudden she stops dancing and carefully lifts up her skirt. What's she doing, what's she looking for? She's wearing white panties, and the next thing you know she's peering into them from above. Oh, very modestly, mind you, she's not the type to be immodest. It's just that the others don't exist for her. She's in a world of her own, and there's something she needs to attend to. The drunks snigger, but she doesn't hear them. She peers inside her panties for a time, and then she lets the elastic snap shut. The skirt falls into place, and she starts whirling again like a slender cloud. What did she see? A young fat guy steps forward and knocks her down. She lands with a thud at the feet of the singers. They stare straight ahead and continue their sacred music without missing a beat. The ladies go on singing, and the man with the harmonica goes on playing. A strange-looking female with dark hair helps the woman to her feet: 'That's no way to treat a woman.' There's a moment of silence.

'No,' says one of the drunks, 'no, that's true, that's no way to treat a woman. And she's a woman!'

The young man begins to stammer, 'I didn't know . . ., I thought . . ., I'm sorry.'

Another fist-fight? An inebriated giant thrusts a meaty finger in front of the young man's nose.

'I said I was sorry.'

Just the one finger. 'But she's a woman!'

The woman dances around the corner and disappears from view.

Sir Galahad begins to stagger. 'Hate,' he says, 'hate is *Scheisse*, shit.'

Aha, hate. I feel compelled to add that hate, hatred, was the main reason I decided, all those many years ago, to take up painting. And maybe it still is. But hatred of what, of whom? I'd like to know.

I could also plan to make a series of paintings called *Feindberührung*: Enemy Contact. I could do that too. But first the series entitled *Preussisch*: Prussian. And later maybe *Mitleid mit dem Feind*: Sympathizing with the Enemy. The Russian dissident Lev Kopelev, now living in the West, was locked up for a long time in his country for sympathizing with the enemy.

'And,' Sir Galahad would like to know, 'hasn't everyone heard the silence that comes from water?' I know what he means. 'And fear. Fear comes from water. Did you happen to know that?' Yes, I did.

'Well,' Sir Galahad says, 'we youngsters, we cadets, are going to make a lot of noise wherever we go. A hell of a lot of noise.'

He falls asleep, against a tree. A chastened Sir Galahad? Tuck a little money in his pocket. It's all he wants. Let him be. He sleeps there every night. Maybe *back then* he watched with a laugh. Peace be with you.

Bourgeois

You're invited somewhere, hello, good evening, you go inside, goodness, what a lovely house, may I take your coat, do have a seat, and sure enough, there's the family pet. Good evening, he certainly is big, isn't he? You're lucky to have such a house, it creaks and squeaks, but before we start talking let me say this: I'd really like to know who used to live in this house, how they lived in it, what it looked like in 1912 or 1926 or 1934 or 1941, what was said here and what it smelled like. I'd really like to know. But I suppose you don't have any idea. I can see that it doesn't interest you.

So now I have to do something I very much dislike doing: I must bow to the inevitable. You see, my hands are tied!

In case you're wondering where I am, I'm in what people used to call a *bourgeois residence*, a house inhabited by the affluent upper-middle classes. Which it isn't anymore.

Berlin still has a fair number of these houses, most of which were built in the late nineteenth century. Rooms with bold measurements and high ceilings. Marble vestibules with solid stucco-work. And maybe a bombastic mural or two. Of course most of the houses were badly damaged during the war and have been done up a bit. Still, they're not the same as they used to be.

The question remains: what did these houses used to look like and how did their occupants live in them?

I've lived in many a house in Berlin, including splendid houses like these, but I was soon forced to conclude that these rooms would never become my own, not even if I were to buy the place. You see, I may be sitting in *their* living-room, but I don't see the garish glow of their interiors, I don't hear their voices. They barely reach me, no matter how hard I try. An intolerable situation.

Contemplating the transitory things in life is melancholy

43

work, but I've apparently never learned another trade. It's a protest against time. Frankly, I can't think of a more useless activity. The minute we human beings started to use our brains we began to brood about the fact that nothing lasts forever. This torment has produced beautiful works of art, since to a certain extent art represents a triumph over sorrow. I'm surprised you didn't know that. Time can make you suffer. Or freedom, or civilization, or god knows what else. Go ahead and suffer if you want.

Just look at those stately rooms and at the people who live in them now. Common folks like you and me. Noisy creatures who have – let's be honest – made a mess of it. Oh, a few of them have managed to spruce up the inside a bit, made it gleaming white and that sort of thing, but it doesn't measure up to the past. Go see for yourself.

We don't belong in these houses. We can furnish them as beautifully as we like, but we have no business there. Oh, we're much more broadminded and enlightened than the people who lived there then. And luckily, we no longer wear such voluminous underwear. But we aren't civilized, we have no style. All we do is make noise. We always seem to be shouting. We?

For the most part, the former occupants were ridiculous creatures with suspenders, corsets and nasty prejudices. They might have had their noses in the air, but that doesn't mean *our* hearts aren't in the right place. Still, they were able to do what we can't do: live in style.

People of that social standing, also called *class*, knew what was proper and what was not. They fitted themselves into fixed patterns, and that made life somewhat simpler. Today's rabble doesn't know anything anymore. They have no guiding principles, no religion and, before you know it, they won't have their high standard of living either. Then what will they do. They've been stripped of everything. Moral certainties, which previously held them in a straitjacket, are no longer within their reach. So they either cast about wildly for a new set of rules or

44

set off on a grim search. As long as they aren't dangerous, I find they have a certain entertainment value. But you've got to keep an eye on them, since they're bound to make a break for it sometime.

So the upper-middle class has been pushed aside by another class. Oh, let us rejoice at this hard-earned social justice. I wouldn't be so flippant if I were you. Perhaps you don't realize how hard life used to be for a lot of people. One fall from a scaffold, and you'd find yourself out on the streets. The elderly among us can still remember the beggars and their desperate pleas. There used to be a man in Amsterdam who rode around in a little trolley shouting: Any spare change for a mason with a broken *ba-aa*-ck? Oh, people would say, there's the chap with the broken back again, it must be such and such a time. And perhaps they gave him a little change, though they didn't have much to spare.

But culture? Sophistication? Instead of the velvety melancholy of the hotels and pensions in Baden-Baden, Marienbad, Montreux or Biarritz, cardboard boxes have sprung up everywhere, bringing the usual squawking hordes along with them. But culture wasn't the answer in those days either, since people were being exploited left and right then too. However, you did have noble ensembles playing everywhere. Not anymore. And you could walk down the middle of the street. It was very dignified.

But let's change the subject for a moment.

Did you think I'd never tire of asking myself *who* and *what* used to be there? Did you really?

When I walk down these boulevards . . . and due to certain circumstances, I've been walking down boulevards a tiny bit more than ordinary streets lately, though I swear I haven't been neglecting the ordinary streets. (That reminds me, what's happened to the alleyways – I mean the back alleys, the slums?) But to get back to the boulevards . . . which, incidentally, is not where these bourgeois houses are located. No, no, the boulevards are lined with mansions that are even more

45

distinguished. But as I was saying . . . when I walk down these boulevards, I wish I could be totally indifferent to the teeming masses that populate them. What business are they of mine?

I should stop complaining. About guilty landscapes as well. What do you mean by *guilty*? Because they watched impassively amid all that human strife? The land and the people had to come together at some point. Why not in a beautiful forest.

It's better to follow the example of one of those beaming trees. It might even add a few years to your life, provided those cowardly organs on the inside of your body do their part.

Oh, I can go on walking around Berlin and asking myself every time I come to a house: what was here before, who used to live here, what did it look like? But it's high time I cut that out. Who gives a damn about the people who used to live here, they're probably all dead anyway. Is there anything wrong with that?

Yes, there is, but I won't elaborate on this hypothesis. I suspect I'd be wasting my breath.

Fragments

MAN: Shall I make a confession? I've never felt as free as I did when I was a soldier during the war. I know it sounds crazy, but it's true. I'd been to university and everything, I could easily have become an officer. And yet I did all I could to remain a common soldier. I had good connections, so at one point I could even have had a room to myself, but I didn't want one. I wanted to bunk with the soldiers. Someone did all the thinking for you, you had no responsibilities. Life was very simple and, oddly enough, that gave you an enormous sense of freedom.

*

WOMAN: I was fourteen when the war ended. Before then I'd been a fanatical Hitler supporter, if you can imagine that. I carried a picture of the Führer around with me morning, noon and night. But every once in a while it'd get mislaid, and then I'd run hysterically through the house screaming 'Where's my Führer, where's my Führer?' If it weren't so sad, you could laugh about it now. My parents had voted for the German National People's Party, so they were against Hitler. A child like me was a real danger. My father listened surreptitiously to the broadcasts from England. I'd come home and say, 'You've been listening to the BBC again,' and he'd deny it. One time I stood in the garden and yelled 'Of course you've been listening to the BBC!' And that while a Nazi official, a *Kreisleiter*, lived next door! For the first time in my life, my father gave me a beating. Everyone in our house was always whispering 'Shhhh, the *Kreisleiter* might hear you.' I must have been ten or eleven when I said to my mother: 'Mama, what's a concentration camp?' I can still picture the shock on her face. She turned pale and said 'Shhhh, the *Kreisleiter* might hear you.' I don't remember her answer anymore, just her look of sheer terror.

*

MAN: The best years of my life were the years right after the war. I was fourteen. I wouldn't have missed them for the world. It was a time of terrible hunger, and yet it was a very positive period. You looked forward to everything, for example each new window-pane or morsel of food. You were happy with everything. There was also a hunger for non-material things. At last, you were free again to do as you pleased – read books, go to the cinema, concerts, whatever. And of course life kept getting better and better. We're now living in an era of over-consumption, in both the material and non-material sense. You can see it in most young people. I can see it in my own children.

*

WOMAN: What I remember of Kristallnacht in 1938 is this: the next morning, I was taking the tram to work – I worked in an office – and I noticed that shop windows had been smashed all over the city. When I saw the mess after the squatters' riots, I was reminded of Kristallnacht. Anyway, on that particular morning, the overall mood was one of depression. The average Berliner wasn't happy with the turn of events. The tram was going along the Kurfürstendamm (the track went down the middle in those days), when the driver suddenly slammed on his brakes and came to a halt in front of a Jewish furrier's. Near Meinekestrasse. The windows had also been smashed in, and the furs were lying there for all the world to see. The driver dashed inside, with a couple of other passengers right behind him. He came back with a fur coat in his hands and drove off. Most of the people hadn't left their seats, but they didn't dare say a word. I didn't either. I didn't say a word.

*

MAN: I went through a really bad patch during my Army days. I was an ordinary soldier in France, and they picked me for a special job because I spoke French. Why not, I thought, it may be

48

fun. Well, it turned out to be interpreting for the Gestapo. I had to do it for a few months, but then a friend managed to get me out of it. It was horrible. I couldn't handle it at all. I was glad to be back at the Front. When the interrogations didn't go according to plan, they used force. That usually meant dumping the prisoners in a bathtub filled with cold water and repeatedly shoving their heads under water. Or taking them off to an empty room and laying into them. I was in the room once when they did that. They were beating the man to a pulp. I still remember the strange thing that happened next. The door was half open, and a Gestapo man was passing by, with a lot of files under his arm. He glanced inside, put his files down on the floor, came into the room and added a few punches of his own. He then picked up his files and continued on his way. Can you understand a guy like that? I have a picture of myself from that period. My face in the photograph is totally expressionless. Dead.

*

MAN: When I was a soldier, I was stationed for a long time in a Russian hamlet. God, those people were poor. I found out that Nazism was no great shakes, but Communism isn't either. We got along fine with those people, we didn't think of them as subhumans, at any rate the blokes in my unit didn't. The Russians are fantastic people, did you know that? They'd share all they had with you. Good-hearted people. But what a system! I showed them a snapshot of my parents and my sisters. You could see our house in the background, a typical house in a typical town, and we weren't exactly rolling in the money. They asked if I lived in that house. Yes, I said. Ha ha ha, they exclaimed, pure propaganda. My mates also showed pictures of their houses, but they didn't want to believe it. Propaganda, they said. They themselves lived in shacks.

*

MAN: I wish they'd stop moaning and groaning about the past, about what those Nazis, those old shitheads, did. I was born after the war, and today's Germany is *us* and not those old Nazi geezers. They're either dead or retired. So what the fuck does that have to do with me?

*

WOMAN: The thing is, it was a bad time, what with the war and all, and when you come right down to it, I suppose none of us were entirely without blame, but it was great to be young!

*

WOMAN: People in other countries don't want to believe that we didn't know about the atrocities. Where I came from, they really didn't know. They were far too naïve. They were just good, decent citizens living a sheltered life. And if they did happen to hear anything, they thought: Germans don't do things like that, that's impossible. Take me – I wasn't interested in that kind of stuff, in politics or whatever. I was young, I was constantly falling in love. The only thing I was interested in was whether I'd had a letter from my boyfriend. That's just the way things were!

*

MAN: During the war I was a staff officer posted to Paris. It's a well-known fact that most of the high-ranking officers in Paris were anti-Nazis. Many of them were involved in the 20th of July attempt on Hitler's life. I was also held for four days by the Gestapo. I knew that several of my French friends in Paris were in the *Résistance*. Still, we were pals in the usual sense. I remember one night, not long after July 20th, a French friend was taking me back to the quarter where I lived. It was late, so the streets were deserted. He grabbed me by the lapels and said: Fritz, I know an address where you can hide. You can go into hiding right this minute if you want. You'll be taken care of. But in those days there was something called the *Sippenhaft*: if one member of a family committed an offence, the rest were held liable. So I said to him, Luc, I said, what'll happen to my wife and daughter? They're in Jena, and they'll be arrested immediately. I can't do that to them. As I recall, we both cried.

Memories

It was summer. He was sitting on the beach, near the water. His father gingerly took the celluloid doll from his hands and threw it far away, into the water of the sea, but it miraculously came back. The sea often brings things back. The child was surprised, and he laughed.

Sometime before World War I, they'd gone to a foreign country, the entire Berlin family and the two nursemaids. That foreign country had been Holland. They'd been in a place called Domburg, yes, that was it, Domburg. Years later he realized he must have been a year and a half old when the incident with the doll happened. Amazing that he could remember it. Then it suddenly occurred to him that perhaps his father hadn't thrown the doll very far away, maybe no more than a few feet, but that the sea had been larger than ever. It's never been as large as it was then.

Similarly, he also remembers his grandfather playing chess with one of his daughters. In other words, with one of his aunts. The game went on for hours and hours. It was deathly quiet in the large, expectant room. Every so often you could hear the rustle of the gardener outside as he meticulously pruned the bushes. Suddenly, one of the chess-players said 'Well, you've touched it now' in a cutting voice, and then it was quiet again for several hours.

The daughter took care of her father for a long time. Her mother died young, so that's why. Many years later she put an end to the old man's life. He was Jewish, and had received notification that he would be deported to the East, but he was in his nineties and bedridden. They discussed it and quickly came to an agreement. She gave him a fatal injection, and there was no longer any need for them to come and take him away. The daughter was allowed to stay: her father was Jewish, but her mother wasn't. She lived to a ripe old age and never regretted her deed. Why should she. She believed she'd pulled a fast one on the enemy. They'd made the trip for nothing and had gone away empty-handed.

He also remembers that when he was a little boy, he and his nanny were sent every day to the reptile house in the zoo. It was right after World War I, coal was in short supply, and they were freezing to death at home. Many distinguished families were entitled to free admission to the zoo, since they were donors. They'd given money for a new pelican or a cheery little bench with feet. So there he sat with his nanny among the crocodiles. It was muggy, it was hot. After a while, crocodiles start to stink.

And the nanny, what happened to the nanny? He doesn't know. Lost touch with her.

You remember things. One quick glance inside, and you find something. 'We are nothing more than ghosts – or memories,' wrote Stefan Zweig. And Jean Paul, the writer from Bayreuth, has said: 'Memory is the only paradise from which we cannot be driven away.' These two aphorisms can come in quite handy sometimes.

He also remembers one of his friends, who lived two houses down the street, asking him in a kind of whisper if he wanted to drop in that afternoon, since his father had a special treat. The father set a wondrous box full of wires and coils on top of the table, and to their great surprise they heard music. Music. How on earth could that be. The father knew: 'It comes through the air.' And at home he told the non-believers: '*It comes through the air.*'

Hadn't the man been talking a few minutes ago about his grandfather? He'd like to tell you more about this grandfather, if you're willing to listen, that is.

At the beginning of the war, he was on leave in Berlin, and he wanted to call on this grandfather to say that when he was in Paris (he was a soldier stationed in Paris), he'd met a girl, a French girl, who was expecting his baby, and had even married her. He wanted to tell his grandfather, but he was dreading it, because his grandfather hated the French. He'd fought against the French in 1870, had even got to the outskirts of Paris. That's how old the grandfather was. So he never talked about 'the French', but about 'the Boche' or 'those damn Frenchies', because he despised the French.

Grandfather, the soldier said, I have something I want to tell you. I met a girl in Paris, I married her and she's expecting my baby. She's French, and she makes me happy. That's what he said, and he meant it.

The grandfather looked at him, and all he said was 'those damn Frenchies'. Nothing else.

Grandfather, said the soldier, if you keep on saying that, I'll never come to see you again. The grandfather stood up and went next door. He came back with a chocolate. Here, my boy, he said. The soldier ate it with great gusto, since sweets like that were hard to come by, and no more was said about the French girl. For the remainder of the short time the grandfather had to live, he never said 'those damn Frenchies' again.

Many other soldiers had managed to marry French girls. These young men were held in great regard. After all, French girls were special.

The man remembers that one day he was ordered to appear before his sergeant. He was on the Eastern Front at the time. There was an *Eastern* Front during World War II, a fact we're not likely to forget. He remembers that this sergeant was a handsome type. Maybe a little on the heavy side, but a favourite with the ladies.

Here, you speak French, you've got a French wife, haven't you? Yes, he did. Good, read me this letter from my wife. It was a letter from his young French wife. It was a long letter, but the wife didn't speak a word of German and the sergeant didn't speak a word of French. Except for *chérie*.

The soldier began to translate: 'Dearest Ulli, I think of you every moment of the day. I long for you so much, I . . .'

Listen, said the sergeant, I don't care about that crap. Skip that part, I don't need stuff like that.

'So I promise that I'll never . . .'

54

Look, get on with it, mate. I said skip it, so skip it. Isn't there anything about a farm or something like that? And he read on: 'I hope from the bottom of my heart that you will soon get some leave . . .'

Cut it out, man. I believe you.

He read: 'This week I went to see my parents on the farm . . .'

That's more like it, said the sergeant. What's it say after that?

'. . . on the farm, and the pig is already very fat. I think it'll be slaughtered next week. My dear Ulli, don't worry, we'll save some for you.'

Good, said the sergeant, that's what I wanted to know. So the pig is going to be slaughtered. You're sure that's what she says.

Yes, I'm sure.

Forget the rest. I'll be eating pork on my next leave, that's one thing I can count on.

He made grunting noises, folded his hands over his stomach and practiced a few chewing motions. The soldier was thanked for his help.

Whatever happened to the sergeant? Killed, of course, about three months after that. He'd just come back from leave.

Oh, what a lot the man still knows. Actually he has nothing special to tell, but it's so hot tonight, so frenzied, that the trains are lurching down the tracks and the houses are sighing.

Fragment

WOMAN: One of my uncles had a top position in a large family-owned firm here in Berlin. But he was half-Jewish, so at a certain moment it looked as if he would have to leave. However, the family who owned the company took him under their protection and saw to it that he was able to remain in his job. I don't remember how they managed to pull it off, but in any case he never had any trouble after that. But then the Russians came, and they wanted to drag him off to Russia because he had a high-level job in the war industry. An officer came to take him away, and of course my uncle tried to explain the situation, about his being half-Jewish and everything. Okay, the officer said, I'll arrange the paperwork so you can stay here, but in return I want to sleep with your wife. And he did. It was my aunt he slept with. Oh God, when I think back to my aunt, a straightlaced lady of the utmost respectability. Yes, my aunt and uncle have been dead for about fifteen years.

Fear

'Frau Neumann is grateful for every day she's still alive.'

'What did you say?'

'That Frau Neumann is grateful for every day!'

'Oh.'

'And yet she does have her ailments.'

'Does she have any ailments?'

'Of course she does.'

'I do, too.'

'Well, Frau Neumann knows that.'

'What did you say?'

'That Frau Neumann knows that, so there's no need for you to say it.'

'Whenever I see a stairway, my heart sinks.'

'Yes, we know you have trouble walking these days.'

An elderly couple sits nearly every evening in a tea-room on the Kurfürstendamm. They stay until closing time, around twelve. Then they slowly get themselves ready for the journey home. The entire trip takes about an hour and fifteen minutes, since they live right up in the north of Berlin, in the Frohnau district. I know, because at one time I lived there too. They used to get out one stop after mine, and then they had about a ten-minute walk.

The entrance to the U-Bahn is right in front of the tea-room, so that helps, but that's just the beginning. They take the U-Bahn to Leopoldplatz, seven stations away, where they have to transfer to the Tegel line, which means going up and down another flight of stairs. It's nine stations to Tegel, the last stop, and then they have to wait around on a windy corner in Tegel for the bus to Frohnau. They're willing to do whatever it takes, just so they can spend hours in the tea-room chatting and sipping and commenting on all that's going on around them.

The man is short and slight, with grey hair combed back from his forehead. He looks absent-minded, perhaps because his hearing is bad, and he's invariably carrying two plastic bags. There are things inside them, but I don't know what.

The woman can no longer hold her head erect. When she hobbles along on her husband's arm, her head hangs down, as if she's trying to look inside her dress. It's less noticeable when she's sitting. She's always grumbling about her husband. Like now. She's talking to a woman who took a seat at their table. Tonight that happened to be Frau Neumann, who does indeed have her ailments, and yet is grateful for every day. She says to Frau Neumann that he, in other words her husband, slams the doors so hard that it nearly drives her insane. Just the other day he neglected to put away his shoes, and he's always leaving the garden gate open, so she's forever having to shut it behind him. He sits wrapped up in his own thoughts. After all, he can't hear a thing.

On the way home, they walk arm in arm, holding on to each other tightly and taking cautious steps. She continues to gripe at him, and he merely says her name from time to time: Erika, oh Erika.

No, she says, you this and you that.

Oh Erika.

Suddenly they're gone, they've left the tea-room. They should be home by now. At least, I hope so. Their places have been taken by two doddering old men who greet each other profusely: one gropes in the air with his hand at approximately eye level (as if it's biting the air), while the other grins and lisps and touches his nose to see if it's still there.

It's no longer evening, but afternoon. This particular afternoon has a stubborn streak. It thinks it can keep the evening at bay. There won't be a warning shot.

In the meantime, the two men have sat down. It takes them a while to get comfortable, but then they talk.

'Well? How did it go yesterday?' asks one.

'Oh, a young girl came and asked: What would you like to drink? I had an excellent beer.'

58

'Really? That's good.'

He wants to pat the other man's arm, but only manages to brush against the sleeve. The arm is so fragile that it remains hidden.

For the rest, they have nothing more to tell each other. They sit quietly staring into space. Every once in a while they smile. They probably know enough. Suddenly the one man stands up; perhaps he's going to address an imaginary crowd. But no, he sits down again. The other one grins and touches his nose.

Dying eagles, who have forgotten how to flap their wings, that's what they are. Keepers of the keys, sworn to secrecy.

I'm almost positive they were young once. They kicked balls and swung, they ran, they jostled others and cursed, they squabbled and pretended, and they wore boots. They did much, much more, but I'd rather you didn't find that out. You can continue to be the one who knows nothing.

Somewhere down the street, there's a large dress hanging in a shop window. It wasn't there before, it's never hung there before. How on earth did it get there? The sleeves turn sternly to the side, as far as they can. They're loath to face the future. I wonder why?

Sometimes these leaden streets suddenly fall quiet, sometimes people suddenly lower their voices. Why is that? If you ask me, they're afraid of something. Maybe. Just what that might be has slipped my mind.

Fragments

MAN: I was in a special unit, the Brandenburger Regiment, operating out of the Intelligence Bureau. Our job was to commit acts of sabotage behind enemy lines. We were dropped in somewhere, and after that we set to work. I blew up three bridges in Russia, right under the noses of the Russians. Three bridges! God, the way they went after us. I mean, they hunted us with dogs. If we survived the operation and returned to our mates in one piece, we were given six weeks' leave. Oh, you wouldn't believe the things I did. I was seventeen and eighteen, and there wasn't anything I wouldn't dare. When I think about it now, I practically shit in my pants. I thought it was a big adventure, and of course I did it for Hitler. Well, we didn't know any better. All the old blokes my age, I mean the ones who were seventeen and eighteen then, who now claim they didn't support Hitler are lying. I tell you, we were ignorant as hell. At the end of the war I was taken to America as a POW, and one day they showed us films about the concentration camps. You know what we did? We threw our clothes and whatever we could lay our hands on at the screen and shouted: Propaganda! Lies! A few days later a clergyman with a number on his arm came to tell us that it was true. From that moment on it was over for us. A couple of men remained Nazis, but we didn't talk to 'em anymore. It was over.

*

MAN: After the war my wife and I started a small business. I had only one employee, a man I hadn't known before. It seems he had a PhD in economics. He was my storeman for several years, and he also did the bookkeeping. I was very satisfied with his work. Whenever he signed his name, he used his title, doctor so-and-so, and that impressed my clients, so I asked him why he was working for me. He seems he hadn't been just an economist, but he'd also been a member of the Nazi party. Not a big shot, just small fry. Still, what happened was this: like most Nazis, he'd had a Jew tucked away somewhere. So this Jew wrote a letter saying that this particular Nazi had saved his life, and that helped his case. After a few years he climbed his way back up the ladder, which isn't surprising, since he had a reputation for being very good in his profession. You need bright people like that. It's true, those Nazis all had a Jew tucked away somewhere, just in case.

*

MAN: Just before the war began I knew a woman from the French Embassy, very prominent in political circles, French down to her fingertips, exquisitely groomed and so on, and she told me that she'd once been seated next to Hitler at a dinner table. She noticed that he was eating vegetarian food and asked him about it. Hitler had replied, '*Gnädige Frau*, the biggest and strongest animals that nature has to offer, such as elephants and rhinoceroses, are strict vegetarians.' She could imitate him so well, we were in stitches.

*

MAN: During the last year of the war I was exempt from military service so I could go to medical school, in Berlin. Do you know what kinds of corpses we had to dissect? Ones without heads. And do you know why they didn't have any heads? They'd been executed. Beheaded. At first it was rumoured that they'd committed major crimes, but later on we realized that some of them were simply ordinary people who had been beheaded for political reasons. You see, a couple of us students went to a session of the *Volksgerichtshof*, the so-called People's Court. It was open to the public. We were horrified. Within ten minutes, that bigmouth Freisler had condemned people to death for really minor things, such as telling a joke about Hitler. We warned all our friends to be extra careful, since you could be beheaded for the slightest offence. For that matter, our professor didn't care whether the corpses had heads or not, just so long as there was a body. Anatomists are happy with every corpse they get, since there's always a shortage. I should know, because I'm an anatomist myself. An older colleague of mine once told me that he used to teach in China before the war, but that he didn't have any corpses. He always drew everything on a blackboard. But for his birthday his students gave him a corpse. He was in seventh heaven. He didn't have the faintest idea where they'd got it, but he did have a corpse.

*

WOMAN: What Hitler did to the Jews was terrible. After all, they're people like you and me. The day after Kristallnacht, I saw a Jew standing in front of his house – I must have been about seven – and the man had put on his World War I uniform, complete with an Iron Cross or some such medal. He kept repeating 'Look, I also fought for Germany, look,' and pointing to his uniform and his medal. I didn't understand much at the time, but that picture has stuck in my mind ever since.

*

WOMAN: I've never forgotten the image of our soldiers fleeing. It was towards the end of the war. I'd just turned eleven, but I thought they were incredibly young, and I felt so sorry for them. Every time I saw a soldier I thought: that could be my brother. You see, I had a fifteen-year-old brother. He'd also been called up to fight, but my mother wouldn't let him go. She hid him. Actually, he really wanted to, but my mother wouldn't let him. She made him hide. He's still alive, and he and I get along fairly well.

*

WOMAN: Before the war my present husband had a house outside Berlin, as a weekend retreat and of course for holidays, and when the air raids started getting worse, he moved his family – he had a very beautiful wife, I'll grant her that, and three darling little girls – to that house. Well, you probably know what I'm leading up to. It happened after a heavy air raid. One of the planes dropped a couple of bombs somewhere outside Berlin, simply because it had a few left or so it could make a faster getaway, or maybe because it had another plane on its tail. In any case, the house was located all by itself in the middle of the woods, and of course the bombs fell right on top of it. The whole family was wiped out. There he was in Berlin, and nothing happened to him. The strangest part is that his house was the only one left standing in the entire neighbourhood. They sometimes say you can't escape your fate.

*

WOMAN: Oh, I know, we Germans are supposed to feel ashamed, to feel guilty. Well, that kind of talk is wasted on me. My father was a man who had to work really hard for a living, and he didn't have time to get involved in politics. Towards the end of the war he was called up and we never saw him again. I had two brothers, one aged seventeen and the other eighteen: both killed. And my mother was repeatedly raped by a couple of Russians, while I, a little girl, had to stand by and watch. Since then, nothing in my life has really given me pleasure. So don't talk to me about guilt. Were my parents and my brothers guilty? Of course not. I'm well aware of what certain Germans did to other people, and I truly regret it, but they shouldn't expect me to feel guilty just because I'm German. I absolutely refuse to.

Autumn

The woman stepped into her car and locked the door. Just at that moment a leaf swirled into the air and hurled itself towards the door in a desperately high arc. Did it want to get in because the woman was so beautiful? In any case, it didn't succeed. The leaf lay down again, in anticipation of the next event.

The leaf's gesture can be seen as the final act of a drowning man. He knows his plea for help has gone unanswered, so he gives up the struggle, goes under, says farewell, waves goodbye.

It's autumn, there's no two ways about it. The leaves are waving.

Ah well, you know how that goes. They hung together on the same branch for a few months, nice and close, and now they're spread out over the wet ground, heaps of leaves lying there, defenceless, hoping for a few kicks. A gust of wind, a footstep: every proposition sends them into ecstasy. Before you know it, they'll be flying off in all directions. Hooligans, that's what they are. Their cheeks flush with excitement, and they inflame many a bush, many a house. The outside wall is smeared with blood from top to bottom. Those who don't know better refer to this as *autumn colours*. Let them. By all means, call them autumn colours. This year's decay is more beautiful than ever.

Some leaves couldn't care less what happens to them. I saw one that let itself fall, plop, right on to a person's chest. The top button of the man's shirt was open, and the leaf presumptuously pushed its way in. Taken off-guard, the man began to sputter and grope inside his shirt; he wasn't going to put up with the whims of nature. I heard him call the leaf a 'nosy little bugger'. He was swearing at it. Good.

Actually, I like the dark Berlin best, the city in black, the slick streets of autumn, when people are in a hurry to get home.

And there they go: gaping, greeting, mumbling, on their way to the next hurdle. Suddenly a barefoot man in swimming-trunks appears in their midst. He has a bow and arrow on his back and is carrying a small burlap bag. He's doing the shopping, he's out hunting. It's drizzling and the wind is blowing, but the man takes no notice. He strides on, his torso gleaming in the rain, without seeing the many eyes which are fixed on him for a brief moment. Hey, a man in swimming-trunks.

In the autumn, sounds suddenly have a little more breathing space. They're no longer so muted, they don't rattle, they get carried off by the wind. Most people stay at home and ask themselves why the sun has disappeared. Not me. I go back to taking long walks and visiting people. In other words: viewing the battlefield and adjusting the borders. Because there are borders.

Borders can be recognized, adjusted, violated. Here's the sand, there's the gravel, and the railway sleepers are over there. Where does the forest end and the camp begin? Where does the meadow end and the city begin? Where does talking end and the scream begin, where the silence and the word? Where does the shrubbery begin, the gleaming river, the deadly blow? Where the grass, where the concrete? There, perhaps, where that ant is struggling with its burden.

During the afternoon the sun pays us a short visit, by way of exception. 'Gute Nacht, sun,' the child in the bus said, 'see you tomorrow.' She kissed the sun, which did shine down on us briefly, since he'd agreed to. But you could tell that he had his mind on other matters, that he was miles away.

The little girl was sitting with her grandmother in the top of a double-decker bus, on the front seat, where you have the best view. The driver, who is seated directly beneath you, takes care of everything, so you don't have a single worry.

The child is singing. All of a sudden she says: 'If you believe in God, he looks after you, doesn't he?'

'He certainly does,' the grandmother answers.

'I believe in God,' the child declares.

'Me too.'

65

'I really, truly believe in God.' And before the grandmother can echo her statement, the child says, 'I'm an early riser,' and continues her song. For the time being the child will feel safe and secure; she goes along with it all. She sings.

I think you should know that reality, the outside world, is bald and sometimes downright revolting, that it's foolish and stinks to high heaven, but that you can always retreat to the cosy rooms of art. But what's that – art as an escape? Yes, of course, why not. 'We have art in order not to die of the truth,' Nietzsche tells us.

But Nietzsche said a lot of things. The words of hotheads like him are subject to a variety of interpretations, like art, like holy scriptures. They can be used to justify the most evil of acts, provided you're hell-bent on doing so. Be my guest.

Art can even be comforting. That too. For example, the sound of music tapping mournfully against the windows can be of great comfort. It confirms our suspicions, it brings the inside and the outside in equilibrium, and that may be a comfort.

Even when darkness closes in around you and the animals do a dance. Even then.

The Woods

I didn't go out looking for a new place, it was offered to me. It's the former studio of Arno Breker. Okay, so who's Arno Breker? He was a sculptor, the one who made those towering statues for Adolf H.'s Chancellery.

It's a yellow brick building of massive proportions, not at all ugly, even though it was built at the end of the Thirties, the beginning of the Forties. It's in a quiet location, just a stone's throw away from the edge of the woods. It was so big that it's been subdivided into several studios. I work there. Where else should I work. The dog was all for it, so that was another reason.

For what's around it. Woodland, lots of it. Grunewald. No, that's not just a municipal park, it's a large forest, with lakes and wild animals.

At night the woods are far from friendly. At night the trees assume a menacing stance. I can see their point. They hurriedly rid themselves of their colours, squeeze themselves into a tight ball, hunker down and become dark fists. Listen to the hooting of the owls. Faint cries.

At night humans don't make their presence known here. Or do they. No, that was an animal scurrying past.

At night the dog and I walk through the frowning woods, along the furtive paths. It's become a habit.

I moved here in January. Because it was snowing, I came to the following conclusion. Freshly fallen snow, draped oh so carefully on the branches, is not beautiful. No, that's the snow of picture postcards and sleigh-bell rides. The kind of snow that wears little white socks. Well, how about the snow that staggers off under the orders of a stern sun? No.

Aged snow, now that's beautiful. Hungry snow in the twilight. Grim, determined, stubborn snow, in an ancient forest. The snow wishes the path were wider, it presses itself against the tree trunks until there's no room for anything else: wherever you go you see snow and tree trunks, lying and standing all over the place. It's remorseless. Woe be unto anyone who tries to flee. Blackness is the only thing that goes with all that white. And fearful people.

This snow conjures up the image of a lonely fairy-tale of long ago, in the cruel East. You get entangled in thrashing tree roots, in a resentful lake. The dead have made room.

So for the moment I'm satisfied. Yet this studio has one disadvantage. There's no U-Bahn to the centre of town, just a bus. I'm sorry about that. I'm quite fond of the U-Bahn. The smell, the hustle and bustle, the echoing walls, the footsteps, the hum of voices. Every time it's made beautiful all over again.

The studio is located in a residential neighbourhood with tall fir trees surrounding the houses. There are scores of new buildings: expensive bungalows and homes owned by elderly couples. Quiet. And everything painted white. Very genteel, in my opinion. White. Makes you think of southern climes. The old German dream of the south, the sun and the Doric column. Let's hope Adolf H. can't see this. He wouldn't approve. According to him, houses with flat roofs were un-German, definitely *verboten.*

There are also villas left over from the old days. Marvellous structures. Grandeur oozing from every pore. They were meant to impress the viewer. They still do, even though they're run-down. There's no reason for envy (these days everyone is envious), since hardly any *rich* people live here. Most of the villas have been transformed into an institute of some kind or another, perhaps a home for repentant artists. Or else there are eight names on the front door. So don't go throwing bricks through the windows, it wouldn't serve any purpose. Rich people no longer live in large houses. They live in bungalows, which aren't as big as the villas were. No one has servants these days. And as for space, well, people had a lot more comfort back then. Almost everybody knows that.

Oh yes, the dog. Well, the dog is quite happy here. At long last, trees again. She has a lot to sniff and do here, quite a change from the human vomit on the Kurfürstendamm.

68

This neighbourhood's crawling with distinguished canines. From time to time I hear the dog yelping girlishly. That happens when she's surrounded by too many gentleman dogs. It sets her to thinking. It strikes her as odd. But as every dog connoisseur knows, gentlemen dogs make allowances for smart little creatures like her. But one day, it was during winter, she was so sick that she no longer cared what the lads thought of her. She was looking for grass, she wanted to throw up.

I get along quite well with that melancholy animal, even though she's recently taken to protesting a little. Don't ask me to elaborate on that. She follows my every move, she keeps tabs on me, I assume she reads what I write. I feel spied upon. If I move my foot an inch, an eye opens in the dog basket. What's he doing, oh, he's moved his foot. Well. The best thing to do is to sit without moving a muscle.

I won't be the least bit surprised if she suddenly starts talking to me tomorrow. A short, but pointed remark. Or else an endless litany of complaints about the way I've brought her up. I won't be the least bit surprised, I promise. We should be able to deal with each other on an adult level. Let her answer the phone if I'm not home. Why should I be surprised?

One day a visitor came. He wanted to talk to me, but he hardly said a word. He watched the dog the entire time, and then remarked that it wouldn't surprise him to hear that she put her false teeth in a glass of water at night. I said she didn't do that, I denied it. I showed him that she still had all her teeth and that she was incapable of picking up a glass, much less filling it with water. No kidding, this conversation really took place. Well, said the visitor, I thought she might, I think she's that kind of dog. No, I said, she's not. He went away disappointed. He won't be back.

Years ago I had to go to Scotland for some reason. While I was there, an elderly lady pointed to a dog in her car, a Labrador, like mine. The dog took my measure, grimly looking me up and down. 'Almost human,' the woman said. And yet it wasn't true. Dogs are animals.

69

Fragments

WOMAN: I'm the only woman in our street who wasn't raped by the Russians. And that's no exaggeration. We had a garden, and I hid in the bushes day and night. The first group of Russians weren't so bad. They even warned us about the ones coming after them. Yes, that's right, they warned us. Well, they came. Most of them were Mongolians. So the story about how they'd suffered at the hands of the Germans and were coming to seek revenge isn't true. Oddly enough, those who'd really suffered behaved differently. My mother and I saw the Mongolians for the first time on the corner of the Teltower Damm. They were accompanied by a couple of Russian officers brandishing whips, like lion-tamers, to keep them in line. We couldn't believe our eyes. But to give credit where credit's due, we also met some very nice Russians. In the end about ten Russians were quartered in our house. They were very good to us. They even supplied us with food. One of the officers always spat on the floor in the hallway, but my mother quickly cured him of that. Otherwise, they were nice people. Very friendly.

*

WOMAN: That there was so much discord among relatives, among families, that's what was so awful under the Nazis. One of our neighbours gave his son a rocket for something he'd done, but the boy was a fanatical member of the Hitler Youth. 'How can you say that to me, Father,' he said, 'I'm in uniform.' The father was so angry he smacked the boy hard on the side of the head, a blow he wasn't likely to forget. Goodness, the number of children who informed on their own parents! By the way, not so long ago I ran into that little boy, though of course he's grown up since then. He just laughs about it now.

*

MAN: When I was a boy in Berlin I hardly ever had any contact with real Nazis. Our next-door neighbours and the entire neighbourhood were anti-Nazi. It wasn't until my mother and I (my father had been called up) were evacuated to Silesia in '43 that we ran into people who were rabid Hitler supporters and still believed that Germany was going to win the war. They weren't half surprised when we told them about the bombing raids on Berlin. Remember, you didn't have TV back in those days. They had absolutely no idea what the situation was really like. Besides, hardly any of them had ever been to Berlin. They couldn't imagine what it was like to live in a big city. It was peaceful in those villages, so countrified, you can hardly believe it now. All right, most of the men were in the service, that's true. But you shouldn't forget that they had enough to eat. And absolute peace. Until all of a sudden the Russians were ten miles away. Their world totally collapsed. The men were either killed or dragged off to Russia, and the rest of the population fled or was forced to leave. It's now part of Poland. Nobody from the old days is living there anymore. Just Poles. For a long time we weren't allowed to visit those areas, but we are now. Oh yes, I go back to the same villages in Silesia every year. As far as the countryside and the peacefulness are concerned, nothing's changed. I keep going back. Out of pure nostalgia.

*

MAN: One of my Jewish friends, Bernard Levi, had a delicatessen in my part of town. One day I went to see him and spent quite a time in the shop talking to him. The very next day I was summoned to Party headquarters. I wondered what was up. To my surprise, they said they were aware of the fact that I'd been in my friend's shop the day before, and they told me that if I knew what was good for me, I wouldn't go again; after all, I had a shop of my own. I was naïve enough to say that Mr Levi was a decent man, and they snapped back, 'There's no such thing as a decent Jew.' Well, that was that. Not long afterwards I saw my friend again, somewhere on Friedrichstrasse, at some party or other. I didn't give it a second thought, but bam, the next day, *the next day*, I was given another warning. They told me flat-out to put an end to my association with 'that man'. Soon after that he emigrated to the U.S.

*

MAN: I was badly wounded somewhere in Poland, during the retreat. I was full of shrapnel, partially paralyzed, you name it. I walked with a stick for years, but it hardly ever gives me any trouble nowadays. Anyway, they took me to a field hospital and put me in a room with the other dying men. They'd given up on me. Which means they might have been able to save me, but it would have taken too long. In the time it took to operate on me they could, say, amputate ten legs. So they left me to die. In the meantime, my parents had been notified and given permission to visit me. Provided I was still alive, that is. They came to say goodbye. But to everyone's surprise, I didn't die. I wrote home to tell them I was still alive, but didn't get an answer. Weeks went by, and I wondered what on earth was happening. Then I received word that they'd been killed in one of those big air raids on Berlin. My entire family had been wiped out. I don't have a single relative left. Father, mother, brothers, sisters, aunts, uncles – all gone. They were dead and I wasn't.

*

MAN: I was already getting on when I was called up for service. I was born in 1901. I hated the army. I was one of the oldest in my unit, but I really had them baffled. You see, I was invulnerable. I was immune to their petty punishments, and I had no desire to be promoted, I wanted to remain a common soldier, so they couldn't get at me that way. Of course I never disobeyed an order, since that could land you in a punishment squad, but I did everything in a very slow tempo. They used to laugh at me. I learned in the army how they systematically break your personality. And yet many consider that to be a blessing. Everything is done for you: you don't have to think, and your food, your clothes, everything is taken care of. When they said: take a bath, you took a bath. You fell asleep on schedule. You didn't have to think anymore, everything was taken care of. I looked upon it as a return to childhood. It offers a kind of security which, oddly enough, agrees with a lot of people. I knew so many people who were anti-Nazi to the core, but they thought army life was wonderful.

*

WOMAN: Let me give you an example of the extent of the terror under the Nazis. My mother liked to sing. She sang in a choir, and she enjoyed it a lot. One night she told a joke, a harmless little joke, to five or six women she trusted in the choir. It went like this: What's the difference between an accident and a disaster? If Hitler's standing on a balcony and the balcony collapses and he gets buried under the rubble, that's an accident, but not a disaster. The next day a couple of men came knocking on our door. She was officially interrogated and everything. Goodness, she was sorry. Our entire family was in an uproar. Luckily, my father knew a judge, who saw to it that she was let off with a heavy fine. For something like that, they usually sent you to a concentration camp. Still, you shouldn't be too hasty in condemning the person who informed on her. People like that were sometimes victims of the Nazi terror themselves. Sometimes they told on others to improve their own credibility. They'd got into trouble and were trying to clear their name.

*

WOMAN: My only son was an anti-aircraft gunner from the time he was fifteen, and after that he wound up in the Waffen SS. No, he didn't volunteer, it just happened like that. He was seventeen when the war ended. He spent five years in Siberia, so he was twenty-two when he came home. Mentally he was a total wreck. The Russians had told him that his parents had been hanged by their heels, with their heads dangling down. I wanted him to go to university, but he just couldn't face it. So then I bought him a farm. Do you know the book by Ernst Wiechert, *The Simple Life*? Well, that about sums it up. I think he has the smallest, poorest and most primitive farm in all Germany. I don't understand the boy. He could have had a totally different life, but there he is riding around on a horse and cart. He doesn't even have a car. I can't decide if he likes the life he's chosen for himself. He must notice that others are better off than he is. We hardly ever see each other anymore. We don't understand each other, and that makes me very sad. I'm alone, but also very, very lonely.

The Portrait

She hardly ever sold a painting, so she decided to do portraits on a commission basis. Portraits that were good likenesses. Her first job was the principal of her son's school. Everyone thought it was his spitting image, and she'd asked him to spread the word that she was available.

She didn't like doing it, but she had no choice.

A few days later, she received a letter from a gentleman asking if she would drop by to discuss a portrait. He opened the door himself, a tall elderly man with black eyebrows that hadn't turned grey yet. She entered a musty, dusk-filled room: the curtains – thin brown curtains – were only halfway open. There were also brown curtains in front of the bookcase. Everything was brown. The furniture must have been more than fifty years old. In the corner was a table with tin soldiers, covered with a thick layer of dust, and the walls were decorated with enlarged photographs of war scenes, soldiers in the snow, seen from the back.

He sat there staring at her. What did he want, he wasn't getting down to business. At first he said very little, but he gradually began to loosen up. He told her he'd been in the army during the war. To be honest, he hadn't been an ordinary soldier, no. You see, he'd been a high-ranking officer. But what did that have to do with the portrait, what did he want of her?

He produced a photo album, leafed through it briefly, without her being able to see anything, and then snapped it shut and set it down in front of himself on a wobbly wooden table covered with dirt and grime. He chatted aimlessly about a variety of topics, including the weather outside. Suddenly he said: I hope it won't upset you if I tell you I used to be in the SS.

Did she know what the SS was?

Yes, she had a pretty good idea.

Did she know what the abbreviation stood for? For *Schutz-*

staffel ('Protection Squad'). It had been an elite corps. Once he'd been proud to be in the SS, but after the war people held it against him, they still did, which is why he'd hesitated to tell her, as she surely must have noticed.

Did she want a cup of tea?

No, thank you, actually she didn't have much time, she still had a few things to do, she had to pick up her son from school.

Oh, that's right, she had a little boy. Maybe a silly question, but was she married? No, she was divorced.

Would she like a little salami, or cheese, or maybe some water-biscuits? He had those as well. No thanks, she was fine.

The room was stifling, she wanted to leave, and she still didn't know what he wanted her to do. She asked him, point-blank, whether she was supposed to make a portrait of *him*.

That wasn't what he had in mind. No, it was like this. He had a son. He was no longer married, his wife had died after a long illness. He'd nursed her throughout, she hadn't wanted strangers taking care of her, and yet she used to be a very sociable type, always surrounded by people. Still, in the last few years of her life, she hadn't wanted to see anyone, just her husband. But that had been quite a while ago, and now he looked after himself, oh, he was pretty good at it, cooking and all that, he did everything himself. Unfortunately, he no longer had any friends. They were all dead, or else had been killed during the war. But that wasn't what he wanted to talk to her about, he'd got sidetracked, what was it he wanted to say, oh, yes, he had a son, he had a son, and that was the reason he'd asked her to come here.

Of course his son had a very different opinion about things than he did when he was young. His son had been a conscientious objector. He even voted for the Greens. He didn't talk to his father very often, they weren't really able to talk. The father had tried once or twice, but the son hadn't made the slightest attempt to listen. Still, they weren't angry with one other. Actually, they didn't see each other often enough. The son avoided his father, the father was well aware of that. He lived here in Berlin, he didn't even know where. Every once in a while, roughly every four or five months, the son suddenly dropped in. He only stayed for about fifteen minutes, but they never quarrelled, no.

Of course he thought about his son quite a bit. You see, it's clear that he, the father, didn't have much longer to live, and he hoped that his son would understand his father better after he was gone, since that's usually the way it goes, isn't it? That's why it would be so nice if his son were to have a large portrait of him.

But hadn't he said that he didn't want a portrait of himself?

That's right, but what he meant was not a portrait of himself as he was now, but as he was when he was young. Taken from a photograph.

He yanked the photo album towards him and opened it.

Look, what he really wanted was to have a large drawing made from this photograph. She should name her price, he was prepared to pay quite a bit for it.

She looked at the photograph. It was taken about fifty years ago. A handsome man, smiling, in a uniform bristling with stars, an Iron Cross, all kinds of decorations. Could you manage to get them all in the drawing? he asked. His son would find the portrait after he was dead. He wasn't to know about it now. Do you feel like doing it?

She took a deep breath and said that it didn't seem to be the right job for her.

Why not, why ever not? her friends said later. What does it matter to you? No, no, she didn't want to do it. She told him she wasn't able to do it, that it was too difficult for her to draw from a photograph. She was able do it all right, she just didn't want to.

He must have noticed that she didn't feel like it, since he suddenly asked her if she were Jewish, in which case he could certainly imagine why she didn't want the job.

No, she wasn't Jewish, but it was too hard for her to make a large drawing from a photograph, she just couldn't do it.

He didn't say much after that. When she got up to leave, he said, you're so tall, how tall are you exactly? She was six feet one, and besides she was wearing high-heeled boots. And your parents, were they also tall? Yes, my father was six feet four.

Aha, then he must have also been one of us?

No, he hadn't been, he hadn't been in the SS.

Oh, he hadn't been? Well. He helped her into her coat and wished her well, but she noticed that he was disappointed. He asked her if she knew anyone who would be willing to do the portrait instead, but she said she didn't. She wanted to leave. She left.

Irene

My new house needed some repairs, and they weren't quite finished. Would I mind living in a flat for the duration, just ten days. Won't it be noisy there? No, it won't be noisy. Are you sure? Yes, I'm sure. Okay.

So there I was standing in front of the block of flats with all my worldly possessions. Before the removals man and I dragged everything inside, I decided to go upstairs and open the front door. The dog went with me. The flat itself was on the fourth floor.

A door opened on the third floor, and a fat, disagreeable-looking male head appeared. Dogs are not allowed in these flats, and if you and your dog don't leave, I'll call the police. You must vacate the premises immediately. Go.

It may be true that dogs aren't allowed here, but starting off by threatening to call the police is not the proper way to go about things. I stood still for a moment, and then unleashed a volley of four-letter words. At moments like these any manners I've ever learned go flying out the window. I know that's wrong, and it sometimes worries me.

I went on upstairs, opened the door and told the dog to wait inside. I'll be back in a moment, why don't you go and read or something. You see, I don't care about the cops, but if the contract stated that dogs weren't allowed in these flats, I was going to have a real problem on my hands. There I'd be, standing on the pavement with all my belongings, looking like an idiot.

Downstairs in the garden I ran into an elderly lady sniffing at the flowers and scratching at the soil. In other words, she was gardening. Do you happen to know who the owner of this block of flats is? Oh, are you the Dutch painter? Welcome. Well, I'd hardly say I felt welcome, since blah, blah, blah, while the dog in question is very quiet and well-behaved, not the type to make a mess on the stairs, and she rarely barks, because she's a melancholy Labrador.

Oh, goodness, Herr Mecke is always *meckern*, moaning, about something. Go on back to your flat. Meanwhile, the dog had come downstairs, because, as she said, it wasn't any fun up there. While I smuggled her back upstairs, the woman had a word with her downstairs neighbour, whose son appeared to be the owner, and the affair was settled within two minutes. Herr Mecke has absolutely no say in the matter. It's true, dogs aren't actually allowed, but we'll have a talk with him. An annoying man, Herr Mecke. Later I heard my rescuer downstairs arguing fiercely with Herr Mecke. How dare you, we Germans have always treated foreigners so unkindly, what on earth must they be thinking of us, you used to have a dog yourself, etc., etc.

Needless to say, I thanked her heartily. I came across her the next morning in the nearby shops and oh, she hadn't had a wink of sleep, all because of that disgusting Herr Mecke. We Germans have a bad enough reputation as it is. Oh, Herr Mecke could be nice sometimes, quite helpful when it came to odd jobs and things of that sort, but my goodness, people like that are never going to change. You mustn't blame him.

Don't worry, I'm not going to try to get even, I couldn't care less about Herr Mecke. I won't say anything if he won't. I didn't tell her that I'd slept very soundly that night, and had even done a little drawing, though it was my first evening in a new place.

A few days later the dog was out playing with a fellow canine. On the pavement, mind you. But that was also forbidden, according to Herr Mecke. He stuck his big fat head out of the window and began to shout. But when I want to I can shout even louder. I thought to myself, if he says one more word I'll run upstairs and throw him out of the third-floor window, but apart from that I'm a very lovable person; I prefer to avoid quarrels. He shut his window and didn't show his face again. For one brief moment I might have felt sorry for him. I no longer remember whether I did, but I might have.

It seems that the helpful lady is named Irene. She does her

shopping on a red sports bike. She's a widow – her husband was a professor of musicology. She still enjoys going to concerts. She can usually get a lift with a cellist who plays in the Berlin Philharmonic Orchestra, which she refers to as 'my Philharmonic'. She's a faithful member of the small white church across from her flat. She says that her belief in God gives her great peace. She's eighty-three years old. She occasionally talks about the past, and it's debatable whether that was so long ago.

'I wasn't a Nazi. I know it sounds awful, and I hesitate to say it. I almost don't dare to, because everyone says he wasn't a Nazi. I know that, but I so hope you believe me. I wasn't a Nazi, I really wasn't. And why was that? Well, certain theological circles were opposed to Nazism from the beginning, and my family was part of them. Even before the war, I was in contact with people who later took part in the 20th of July plot against Hitler. Some of my relatives had been in a concentration camp, so we knew all about them.

'I so hope you believe me, it's really true. *It's almost awful to say that you weren't a Nazi.*

'One day at work I was ordered to go along with about twenty other women to a street that was later renamed "Strasse des 17. Juni". Hitler was supposed to go by. We were told to stand there and cheer.

'I tell you in all honesty, and I hope you believe me, I didn't look at him when he passed by. I didn't see him, really and truly I didn't. So I've never seen Hitler.

'In our home the radio was always switched off when he was speaking.

'Even before '33, I was employed as a kind of social worker by a couple of large companies. They had built public housing estates and model settlements on the outskirts of Berlin for their workers. They didn't want their employees living in slums. But these people had never lived in the country, so my job was to show them how to keep geese and things like that. I'd been given a training course, which naturally included cooking and nursing too. Most of the workers who lived there were Social

Democrats, but there were also a few Communists. Some of them had been in concentration camps, and they told me all about them. The intimidation tactics worked, because they kept pretty much out of sight. But there were a few Nazis as well. In '36 or '37, when the Nazis took over everything and we were all made to toe the line, I had to work with two of these Nazis. At that time the whole country was geared towards rearmament.

'They were aware of my views, but oddly enough I was allowed to go on working. I didn't have to join the party, nor was I pressured to sign up for the Nazi women's organization. I was simply allowed to go on working. Every so often I had to meet with those two Nazis. One was nice and not at all fanatical, and the other was what we used to call a real Nazi. He was insanely pro-Nazi, but for some reason he liked me, so he left me alone. I still remember the three of us sitting around after the first meeting. I said jokingly: And now I suppose it's time to sing the Horst Wessel song. The other man kicked me on the shin, but the real Nazi didn't bat an eyelash. Oh, I said some really terrible things to him, for which I could have been thrown into a concentration camp, but I wasn't. People were terrified of him. When the Russians were just outside Berlin, no one dared to hang out the white flag because he forbade them to. He threatened them with capital punishment if they did. He was a fanatic to the last.

'The Russians dragged him off, and he starved to death in a camp. His wife is still alive, a terribly nice, helpful kind of person. Makes you wonder, doesn't it? A woman like her saddled with a madman like that.

'One day towards the end of the war, a friend of mine asked me if I was afraid of the Russians. I still remember my answer. No, I said, I'm not scared, I'm not anything, I'm incapable of having feelings. I was totally numb. Well, he replied, the Russians scare me to death. The next day he was dead. He'd tried to protect his wife and two daughters. He, a man who'd survived several years in a concentration camp and who'd more or less spent the entire war hiding in his own home. He was forced to watch for hours while his wife and daughters were being raped. And then afterwards he was shot to death in his own garden. The women buried him there. A man who'd opposed the Nazis from the very beginning.

'Tragic things like that happened quite often. Guilty or not, if your time was up, you got it in the end. I knew women who were Communists, who'd been in hiding, and yet they were raped repeatedly when they were finally "liberated". It must have been a great disappointment to them. They could say: I'm a Communist. But then the Russians would reply: Yes, that's what they all say. Well, they were right about that.

'They were very primitive, the Russians who were brought here to rape and plunder. Most of them were Mongolians. For example, they didn't know how to use a toilet. They destroyed things because they didn't know what to do with them. They thought everyone who didn't live in a slum was a capitalist.

'One time they came to our house. I was living with one of my aunts. They always shouted, *Frau, Frau, heraus, heraus!* – woman out. One of those soldiers, I can still picture him, stood looking at us with big brown eyes. He couldn't keep his eyes off us. Suddenly he said something that obviously meant: Come with me. We had to go. He locked us up in the basement. We were scared out of our wits, but he threw the key in through the window. He rescued us, he saved our lives! I'll never forget it.

'Not long ago a friend of mine, a woman I go out and do things with, told me that during the war she had been evacuated because of the air raids, and she wound up somewhere in Silesia, near Auschwitz. She didn't know exactly what was going on there, but she heard people talking and she saw the transports. In other words, she heard and smelled enough. She made it clear that she was determined to go back to Berlin, absolutely determined.

'Once she was back in Berlin, she said to her friends: Something's going on there, we don't know exactly what, but something's going on there, something terrible. A few day later she was picked up for questioning and interrogated for hours.

She was told that if she ever said another word about what was going on there, she'd be put in a camp where she'd have to work until she died.

'I'm only telling you this to illustrate how strong the reign of terror was. You had to be on your guard constantly. Young people sometimes ask us whether we couldn't have got together and done something. They don't understand how widespread the terror was. Recently, my friend's son asked him that same question, and he replied: Perhaps your children will later ask you why you didn't do anything to keep the Wall from being built.'

Fragments

WOMAN: During the Nazi period entire blocks of flats were sometimes knocked down to make way for new ones. The Nazis did a good job of organizing that. You received a letter at home, telling you that you had to vacate your flat before such and such a time, and you were immediately given a list of empty flats. You could take your pick. I know, because it happened to my mother. I went with her to look at potential flats. And do you know what kind of flats they were? Those belonging to Jews. They hadn't even been evicted yet! They were still living there! I said: I'm not going with you anymore, you can go by yourself. You're a member of the party, you voted for Hitler, I didn't. But my mother didn't want to either. Flats with the Jewish occupants still in them – she thought that was too crazy for words.

*

MAN: The Polish campaign had begun, and I was still at grammar school, in the last year but one. We were told that if you volunteered to fight, they'd give you your school certificate straight off. We were raring to go, to be in Poland. Oh, the young are so reckless! If you wanted to get into the action fast, you had to join the Waffen SS. I was so curious, and I thought I'd have a couple of months of war and adventure. Well, it cost me six years of my life. Six years at the Front. A large part of it as an officer. An officer in the Waffen SS. I was wounded three times, but I survived. I know you're thinking, oh here's another one. But you're wrong. I'll tell you straight out that we were misled and misused, that we were made to commit criminal acts. I'm now 100 per cent against it, though I can't really say I was for it in those days – we fought, and we didn't have time to think about things. Still, I don't want to let my fellow soldiers down, so I go to all the reunions. But I make no bones about the way I feel. Can you understand me, just a little?

*

WOMAN: I was around eleven years old when I went to Munich with my parents to see the *Entartete Kunst* (Degenerate Art) exhibition. Except that I wasn't allowed to go inside. You wouldn't be interested, my parents said, so why don't you wait outside. When they came out, they said: It's a good thing we didn't let you go in, because those paintings were really ghastly. My parents were real philistines. You can imagine what they saw there: Beckmann, Kirchner, Nolde, you name it. And they thought it was ghastly! I only came in contact with that kind of art after the war, and I revelled in it.

*

WOMAN: Oh, you foreigners don't know the first thing about National Socialism. Here's something else you won't understand: my father was an anti-Nazi and he was in the Resistance, he really was, and you want to know why? Because the Nazis promoted the cause of the workers, and he was opposed to that. You foreigners don't know that, do you, that the Nazis did so much for the workers. Health care, housing, concerts, holidays, every-thing. You don't want to believe it, do you. And yet it's true. My father was against all that. He didn't support the workers. I do. Fortunately I'm not like my father. I'd rather have peace.

*

MAN: My parents were in a difficult position during the Nazi period. They were anthroposophists, followers of Rudolf Steiner. I'd always attended Rudolf Steiner schools, but, as you know, they were banned by the Nazis. Still, that didn't stop Nazi bigwigs like Goering from shopping in our place. They'd patronized my parents' shop for years, because it had been in business since the last century. But after a while all the big orders went to our competitors. And why was that? Because they were members of the Nazi party. My father then felt compelled to apply for membership. He was *not* accepted. *Not* accepted.

*

MAN: Ah well, Germany was just as big before the war as it is now; or rather, the world was just as big. I came from a village, and most of the people had never been any farther than their own village. Berlin, for example, was far, far away. There was this farmer's boy, and he'd gone to Berlin for some reason, I don't remember what. My, oh my, oh my. The next day his father said to him: Go and lift the potatoes. And the son said: Yesterday I was in Berlin, and today you want me to lift potatoes. No, that's impossible. Since then he was known as The Berliner. That's what he was called to his dying day. Not that he lived very long. He was sent to Russia during the war and never came back. Missing in action.

*

WOMAN: I witnessed quite a few of the street fights between the Nazis and the Communists here in Berlin. I was the inquisitive type in my younger days, so I always managed to find a place in the front row. It was terrible, people were getting killed every day. But don't go bringing up 'those poor Communists' with me. They were brawlers, just like the Nazis. They weren't one whit better. The only difference is that the Nazis were on top for a while, so suddenly the Communists were heroes. And now the Communists are back in fashion. Whenever anyone talks about the Resistance, it's the Communists this and the Communists that. After the war all we ever heard about was the 20th of July conspiracy against Hitler, and now the Communists get the credit for everything. But they're forgetting the actions of all those anonymous, apolitical, religious or non-religious people and groups. Oh, these trends can be so depressing.

*

WOMAN: I recently met a Jewish woman who said to me, 'In a certain sense, it was much more difficult for you Germans than for us Jews. Despite all our suffering, it was actually fairly simple for us: we were being persecuted. We didn't have to choose. It was much harder for you Germans, since you had to spend twelve years examining your consciences, asking yourselves how you should behave, whether this or that was acceptable.' Don't you think it's wonderful that a woman who's been through so much could bring herself to say something like that?

The Nose

I met a man, and by god, what a nose he had! It looked like somebody had been throwing everything but the kitchen sink at it for years. Had another guy once grabbed him by the nose, pulled it out about ten yards and let it bounce back? His nose was not only conspicuously large, it was also covered with scratches and bumps.

I thought: I can keep on staring at that nose, or I can ask him how it came to be like that. So I asked him how his nose came to be like that.

It's funny, the man said, but nobody ever dares to ask me that. Everyone stares at it, and I hear them thinking, what's up with his nose, but nobody ever asks. I'll tell you something, but I warn you, it's going to make you laugh: just this week I got my big nose caught in the door.

See what I mean, you're laughing. I'm just grateful it wasn't my head. I opened the door, and someone else banged it shut. I stuck my head around to see what was happening on the other side, 'cause I'm the curious type, and that's when my nose got stuck. You should have heard me.

Try to imagine, the man continued, try to imagine my nose without all the gashes and lumps. If you can manage that, you'll have to agree that it's a whopper. Always has been. Got it from my mother.

The funny thing is that my nose and I came out of the war without a scratch. It didn't get bashed in with a rifle butt, it didn't get driven over by a tank, it didn't even get frostbitten.

Early on, I made up my mind that when I fell in love with a girl, I was going to take a good hard look at her nose. She had to have a small nose. I wanted kids with a normal nose. But no, nothing of the kind. I've got three kids, and all three of them have a conk like mine. One look in the cradle and I could tell it was going to be a disaster.

At the beginning of the war I married a gorgeous girl. She had a small nose. To tell you the truth, I never understood what she saw in me, with a nose like mine, but anyway the marriage didn't work out. Only a few weeks after I left for the front she found someone else, a Frenchman, sent to work in a factory here in Berlin. A guy with one of those pointy noses. Really – I found a picture. I could understand her having another man then, but she kept it up after the war, and I couldn't forgive her for that. The way I saw it, she had to put a stop to it some time. So I packed my bags and left. Fortunately we didn't have any kids. I never saw her again.

My present wife is also a beauty. Funny, isn't it? I'll bring her along the next time so you can see her, and you can tell me honestly whether or not you think she's beautiful. She's got a tiny little turned-up nose. To this day, she's still a knockout. I can spend hours looking at her. But there you are, all three of our kids have big noses. They blame me for it, and I can hardly say it isn't my fault.

Still, two of them, my two daughters, are married. If you want my honest opinion, their husbands aren't exactly slouches in the nose department either. Not as bad as ours, but still good-sized beaks. So I fear the worst for their children. They don't have any kids yet, but they're working on it. I tried to warn them, I said: Do you really think you ought to do that to a kid. But they don't care. My daughters have forgotten how much they hated it when they were little. They're determined to have kids. So then I had a word with my sons-in-law. They don't give a hoot either. It's not like it's some disease, they said. In that respect, young people today are pretty easygoing.

When I was in the army, they were always giving me a bad time about my nose. The enemy was advancing, but they still found time to make jokes: Heinrich, why don't you block that one with your nose so we can keep on playing cards. I'll never forget it, fifteen minutes later the joker who said that was dead.

Yeah, I saw a lot of blokes get killed. Blokes you hung around with day in, day out. And to think I survived. Most of them thought they were fighting for a better world. What did we kids know about concentration camps?

Before the war, I simply couldn't understand how someone could be against Hitler: things were getting better every year, and there was a real feeling of camaraderie.

What bothers me most are all those mates of mine who didn't make it. I admit, sometimes when I'm alone, I think of those guys and shed a few tears. Pure sentiment on my part, I suppose. Listen, it's not like I sit around bawling my eyes out every day! No, that's not what I mean. It happens maybe once every two years. Though the last ten years or so it's been happening more often. Before that, it used to hit me maybe once every three years.

Now you're going to say, why doesn't he weep for the victims of Nazism? Well, the answer is: I didn't know any personally. For example, I never saw a Jew when I was growing up. There weren't any in our village.

Whenever I read or hear about the victims, I feel a surge of compassion. And shame too. But right away my thoughts stray to those dead mates of mine. Isn't that weird? I can't help it, that's just the way it goes. And I know why it happens: *it bothers me that they don't know what I know.*

They don't know what they died for. They thought they did, but they didn't. I do, 'cos I just happened to survive.

As long as I'm at it, I suppose I might as well go on. You see, I'd really like to tell them the truth. About how we were living in a world of make-believe, stuffed full of phoney ideals. Which, by the way, I notice is often the case with young people. That fanatical adherence to phoney ideals.

I wonder: Do the dead stay stuck forever in the ideas they had then, or do they keep on learning? Do they know what the score is now, or do they still have the same thoughts? Can the dead think? Every now and again, questions like these go running through my head.

But I've got sidetracked. I was talking about my nose. I'd rather talk about my nose than the war. You see, you start talking about a nose and you end up talking about life after death.

I've begun to wear glasses in my old age. I was happy with the glasses. I thought they'd draw people's attention away from my nose. Wrong. Too bad about the glasses, everyone said, they make your nose stand out even more. I spent a week wondering whether I should wear them. But then I went to pick up the dog and found I was trying to grab hold of a bush instead, so I decided to keep the glasses.

And now this accident with the door.

It's all the same to my wife, she's never complained about my nose. She thinks of me as the quiet type, and she likes that. And I am. I am. Except for those times when I burst into tears. Otherwise, I'm pretty quiet. Yeah, I'd say I was. Yeah.

Donnerwetter

Walking through the woods near my house, I hear the wind blowing through the trees, I hear the trees creaking, and it does me a world of good.

Sometimes the trees even scratch and scrape, as if their growth rings are made of iron, which they're not. Why they scratch and scrape is beyond me.

I hear the rat-a-tat-tat of the woodpecker and wonder whether his neck ever gets sore. Okay, let's suppose it does. Wouldn't he have to undergo treatment? What would the procedure be? Would he have to lie down, with his skinny little legs stretched out? No, no, the woodpecker wouldn't have to lie down. I think they can treat necks while you're sitting down. You just have to bend your head over the table. But what'd happen to his beak? After all, his beak would get in the way. Would they have to make a hole in the table for his beak? You see, all kinds of questions start running through your head when you listen.

But if the wind is willing I can sometimes also hear the distant roar of the town, where there's a lot of moving to and fro, a lot of hustle and bustle. You can hear it from here.

If you've never been in a big city, there's one thing you should know: so many strange things are going on, often at the same time, that it's impossible to keep up with them. Oh, I know that, but I never stop to think about it.

While merry peals of laughter ring out in one room, the loss of a loved one is being mourned in another. That can happen. There isn't much we can do about it. Those who are now mourning and thinking that life has no more meaning have also done their share of laughing. They've even licked their chops and stuffed their faces while in some far-off place a person was lying down on the street to die of starvation. Maybe this is why people say life is *exciting* or life is full of *surprises*. I look around me, and they're right. Life is full of *surprises*.

93

A lot is going on. Here, in the woods, the woodpecker wipes the sweat from his brow, and a few miles away a car comes to a sudden stop because a light at the end of the street turns red. That's an agreement people have made: you have to stop when a light turns red. If you don't, you get fined. That's why they do it.

The inevitable concurrence of events. Someone once told me that he was terribly upset by a mining disaster. He listened to the reports, pored over the papers, and even shut himself away so he could imagine how the unfortunate miners might be feeling at that moment. How they were trapped, and no one could come to their rescue. How terrible it all was. He was totally involved in the disaster. And yet, *at the same time*, a cheery little tune kept running through his head and he couldn't get it out, no matter how much he thought of those poor people deep in the earth.

Every once in a while I allow myself the liberty of sitting around the house and staring at sketches for hours on end in hopes that I'll suddenly know which painting is going to present itself, which painting wishes to be painted. And I grant this wish. With all my heart even. But somewhere else in this dishevelled city another insignificant event is taking place. At the same time. I need to remember that.

For example, I know that here, at this very hour, a song is being sung in some nightclub. A big hit in wartime Berlin. It's called *Donnerwetter* and goes like this: 'Gosh darn it! Gosh darn it!, We're bruisers, lalapaloozahs, The gosh darn best of the bunch!'. They used to sing it a lot in those days. That's why you still hear people singing it from time to time.

This stirring number was no doubt being sung somewhere when a couple of men, the kind referred to as workers, came across the body of a dead woman. She was lying in a storage area between a couple of houses. Later on it turned out that she was eighty-five years old. Her neck and face showed signs of injury, her shoes lay some distance away and her body was only partially clothed. The police naturally assumed she was the victim of a crime or foul play.

But what happened was this. The woman had fallen down on

that spot five days earlier and had died instantaneously. Or maybe it was the other way around; nobody knows. Her body was found by a couple of ten- or eleven-year-old kids. They didn't tell anyone, but every so often they removed an article of clothing, threw her shoes away and took what little money was in her bag. It seems the injuries to her neck and face had been incurred at an earlier date, when she'd suffered a similar fall.

She hadn't been murdered. The kids had simply played with a corpse.

The moment the woman fell, somewhere in Berlin someone was no doubt saying: I like it here in Berlin, I like it a lot. That someone might have been me.

I still like it in Berlin. Especially in the winter, when most people take refuge indoors, huddling around their stoves and moaning because the sun refuses to shine. Winter wants everything to be black. Winter unleashes the night, sending the night down upon us, and the night drives out the day. The night is bold and daring.

The days were sombre. There wasn't any sun, the clouds were in a state of confusion, it was a shambles.

In Strindberg's *To Damascus*, the character called The Unknown says: 'Have you ever noticed that before the sun rises, we humans shiver and shudder? Can it be that we are children of the darkness, since we tremble when we face the light?'

Do modern city-dwellers still dare to tremble?

When a patch of blue appears, and the sun peeks warily out to take stock of the situation, all hell breaks loose. I suddenly have no trouble imagining that at this time of year people used to dash off to their country places. The firmament's blue apparel seems to have a disastrous effect on young men. All of a sudden they start their vehicles with a roar, and the hideous blare emanating from within is a torment to the sensitive pedestrian, who decides that when he's grown up and in charge he will only issue driving-licences to men past the age of fifty. With one or two exceptions. Oh, the hubris. Winter has only just left the room.

Fragments

WOMAN: My father was also in the SS. Though not all the way to the end. They threw him out, because he refused to give up his church membership. He wanted to remain a member because his wife (my mother) was a devout Catholic. After he was dead I asked my mother why he'd joined the SS when he was eighteen. My mother told me she'd once overhead a conversation between her mother and my father. Her mother had asked him why he'd joined the SS, for goodness' sake. You know what his answer was? That he looked better in black than in brown. My mother was sure he meant it.

*

WOMAN: We lived near a big SS barracks. On the corner of the street was a bookshop, owned by a small, hunchbacked man. He always had Nazi books displayed up front, *Mein Kampf* or something like that, for the boys from the SS who passed by there every day. To tell you the truth, they were tall, handsome young men, with nicely fitting uniforms, or at any rate we girls thought so. But in the back room he kept books that had been banned. He was also a very wise man. Whenever my father was at his wit's end, he went to the bookshop, and he invariably came home in better spirits, once again full of hope. The bookshop owner had an assistant, a tall, dark-haired Swiss woman. We thought she was a relative of his. After the war we found out she wasn't Swiss at all, but Jewish. She'd got hold of a Swiss passport, and had gone underground in his shop. Right under the nose of the SS. Things like that happened.

*

MAN: I was a soldier somewhere in Bohemia when the war ended. Well, what were we supposed to do? Head home, of course. Or try to. That meant walking hundreds and hundreds of miles, and trying to keep from falling into the hands of the Americans or the Russians, since they'd throw you into a POW camp. One day you'd hitch up with a group of ten men, and the next day there'd be only two of you, but we all got on really well. We helped each other where we could. And I don't mean just the soldiers from the Wehrmacht and the Waffen SS, but also tons of prisoners from the concentration camps. We all travelled together, and there was a real camaraderie. You probably won't believe me, but there was absolutely no animosity. We shared everything we had with each other. It may seem hard to understand now, and yet it's true. Actually, when you think back, that was really strange.

*

MAN: No, I've never felt the need to see the blokes who were with me at the Front again. Even though we went through some pretty rough times together near Leningrad. We were in the Artillery. Oh, you know how it is. They were mostly oiks, if I may use the term, and it was nearly impossible to have a conversation with them. The only subject they could talk about, or ever wanted to, was sex. Because of my schooling, I was soon made an NCO, and my promotion had to be celebrated with the other NCOs, all older, hardened professionals. And wouldn't you know, after the second or third glass they started off on their favourite theme. So, they said, now it's time for our new NCO to tell us about all the women he's laid. Well, I said, I'm afraid I'm going to have to disappoint you gentlemen. I may be nineteen, but I've never got that far. God, was I ever sorry! After that night, they never took me seriously again. Anyone else would have told the biggest lies, but I was stupid enough to tell the truth. I was very naïve then, and to be honest, I still am. I'm always saying the wrong things.

*

MAN: Yes, one time I was more or less indirectly a witness to something that was going on there in the East, behind the front lines. I mean that . . . well . . . ah . . . that groups of Jews were being shot to death. We got there just after it had happened. Women, little children, everyone. But you know the strange part is that we young boys didn't blame it on Nazism. I remember that we all thought, what a bunch of bastards, those guys who did it, and wondered why their superior officer hadn't put a stop to it. After all, our officers had always been real gentlemen, and they made sure that the men behaved themselves, that nothing was stolen from ordinary people, that nobody was raped. They kept a close eye on things. And imposed severe punishments. We got along really well with the Russian civilians. We were quartered in their homes, really nice people. Of course we thought Communism was bad, because we could see that they were living in extreme poverty. Compared to them, poor working-class Germans like me were rich. I tell you, they were glad to see us Germans. In the beginning they treated us like liberators. But later on, because of all that slaughter, they began to hate us more and more.

*

MAN: Right after the war I worked a while for a kind of peace foundation, an organization of pacifists. I was apparently an idealist in those days. Well, if two people a month joined our group we thought we were doing famously. Nobody wanted to think about such things. The war was over, there was peace, and all they were interested in was rebuilding their lives and earning money. So I left.

*

MAN: Six months before the end of the war I'd taken my exams and left school, so they made me an officer. I was part of what you might call the last elite: we were to be Germany's salvation. What a laugh. They shipped us to Berlin as soon as they could. Our job was to defend Berlin. The Americans were somewhere to the West and the Russians to the East. And there we were running back and forth between them. I mean it, all I ever did was march from West Berlin to East Berlin and from East Berlin back to West Berlin. My feet were a bloody mess. Ha ha ha. At least our company commander had some brains. He said: Anyone who wants to go home can go. But no, our brave heroes didn't want to leave. We'd been told to defend Berlin and that's what we were going to do. Ha ha ha. Less than a week later my mate and I were sitting in a trench, with the bayonets on our rifles, and I went to signal my men to attack, but they were all gone. Not a single one was left! Not one! So we got the hell out of there too. God, the whole thing was a farce.

*

MAN: As a boy I despised everything to do with the army, it's just my nature. There's no way I would have joined the army, I can tell you that. I'd rather have been shot. I hated the idea. Towards the end of the war (I was sixteen at the time) I was stopped one time by a couple of 'watchdogs', that's what we called the MPs. They asked me why I didn't have a weapon. In those last few months every male of conscriptional age was supposed to be either armed or in uniform. I could have told the truth and said that our town hall had run out of weapons, but I was cocky enough to say: What's it to you? They wanted to shoot me right then and there, in the courtyard near my house. Just as they began to take aim, an older Wehrmacht officer came along, and he yelled: Hey, you there, are you reduced to shooting schoolboys these days? Well, they said, he doesn't have a weapon and he was insolent. While they were standing there arguing, a plane flew over. Bombs started falling, so I took the opportunity to make a quick exit when everyone was ducking for cover. And I didn't fall into their clutches again.

Nazi

A Nazi. What is a Nazi, actually? Who was a Nazi back in those days?

You have to get used to the way Germans use the word *Nazi*. It took me a while, but I've more or less worked it out. Sometimes you hear old people talking to each other about so-and-so. He was a real Nazi, they say. They don't mean he was a member of the Nazi party, since that didn't necessarily make someone a bastard. Of course it didn't. They mean he was a diehard, a fanatic. You had to watch out for those types. They were champing at the bit to inform on you.

That's gradually what Germans have come to mean by *Nazi*. Time has encroached on the word, it's covered with moss. Time does march irrevocably on.

Who was a Nazi?

When someone says, I wasn't a Nazi, he doesn't mean he refused to carry out orders or that he was a saboteur. It usually means he thinks he wasn't a fanatic. In other words, he wasn't a real Nazi.

There were those who claimed to despise the Nazis, but jumped for joy when their fellow Germans captured Paris. They were 'patriots' and not 'Nazis'. Do try and keep the two separate. It's a fairly complicated business. But we have to make it as complicated as we can for ourselves, since that's the only way we can ever hope to approach the truth.

Anything can happen. How many non-Nazis played a dirty trick on their inferiors, merely because they were allowed to wear a cap and couldn't resist the normal human tendency to pull a fast one on their fellow human beings.

And then there were those who didn't like the Nazis because they were *common*. They equated Nazism with socialism. I know it's hard to believe, but it's what thousands of people thought. All that exaggerated enthusiasm for the workers. In that sense they were right: the Nazis were clever, they paid lip-service to the workers' cause. You're not supposed to say that aloud, but I'm going to anyway.

They saw to it that people had *joy* in their work. They improved the health care system, brightened up factories with flowers and plants, set up 'rest centres' for mothers, organized concerts in factories and arranged for groups of workers to go on luxury cruises to the Mediterranean, the Caribbean or the North Cape. That was no small accomplishment. They didn't have things like that in Russia, which is why so many Communists became Nazis, though they don't like to be reminded of it now.

After years of living from hand-to-mouth, people eagerly lapped up slogans such as 'Common interest before self-interest' and 'No more hunger and cold.' The notion of 'Workers and intellectuals uniting to make Germany strong' was enormously appealing.

The Nazi brand of 'socialism' made a big impression on many *simple* folks. They still talk about it to this day. This is why Communists prefer to avoid the term 'National Socialism', which contains the word 'socialism', and to call it 'Fascism' instead.

In one of his books, Walter Kempowski writes that the terms 'Fascism' and 'Fascists' came into fashion after the Russians captured his home town of Rostock. The first time he heard it, he thought: Hey, that's funny. After all, we aren't Italians. How come they're calling us that?

So far I've neglected to mention the petty informers, the anonymous types who wrote a letter, licked the envelope shut, stuck a stamp on it, pulled on their smelly shoes, slammed the door behind them and hurriedly slipped the letter into the box. And all that to bring disaster down on someone else's head. To me, they're the most repulsive creatures on earth, but they do exist. Not only do they exist, but they're still licking postage stamps with their revolting tongues.

Don't let yourself be taken in by Germans who say they were in the Resistance. Much of the time that can be chalked up to pure bravado. Or maybe not. Because in a totalitarian state every little thing was (and still is) considered to be an act of resistance. If you stuck your arm out and said 'good morning' instead of 'Heil Hitler', you were practically a member of the underground.

What if they'd won the war? According to Erich Kästner, if the Nazis had won the war, they would have had their hands full: all of Europe, from Sicily to the North Cape, would have been one big prison camp, with the Germans standing guard day and night to keep the conquered nations in line. A virtually impossible task.

How old are they actually, the people from those days? The ones who made a conscious choice back in 1933. Let's say they were twenty-three years old at the time. That means they were born in 1910, which puts them in their eighties now. My guess is that they aren't very active any more.

The group with the most loose ends is formed by those who happened to be around thirteen in 1933, which made them nineteen when the war began in 1939. They went through it all, they cheered and waved and marched. Whether or not they did it voluntarily, whether or not they enjoyed themselves, whether or not they emerged unscathed.

Who was a Nazi, who was on the wrong side? Wrong side? I know people who were on the *wrong side* in the 1950s, but that's not what I want to talk about now.

So the older generation no longer knows for sure who or what a Nazi was. The younger generation, which didn't go through it, does know. They know exactly how one should have behaved, which is why they watch the older generation like a hawk. Even I am guilty of doing that sometimes, much to my regret.

If I may take a moment to digress. It looks as if I'm protecting the older generation. Perhaps that's because they've been purified a bit by time. That can happen. Time can make a person incredibly innocent. Time can change a wolf into a lamb. Time can do a lot it shouldn't be allowed to do.

For example, take a good look at the genial old pensioner in that convalescent home. Back then, he used to kick the hell out of anyone who got in his way. I remember it as if it happened yesterday. Now he's an endearing old codger who wouldn't hurt a fly. He too has been encrusted with kindliness by time. He's been transformed. You wouldn't recognize him.

Should a man like that still be punished?

I don't know. I'm supposed to know, but I'm not sure. I've forgotten, it's slipped my mind. Please don't ask me again.

Dogs

Since I live on the outskirts of a large wood, I often run into dogs. They go for walks there. They usually have a person with them.

I've met one who's called Wilhelm. What's so special about that? Well, only that the dog was walking in the woods with a woman, and when the walk was over, the woman wanted to get in her car, but the dog hadn't finished, so the woman kept calling 'Wilhelm komm!' louder and louder, but the dog didn't want to come, and though the woman was starting to get desperate, Wilhelm didn't even look up.

Now what.

So the woman yelled, 'Wilhelm, *auf Wiedersehen*,' pronouncing each syllable one by one. Wilhelm came immediately.

I know that meeting a dog called Wilhelm is not the thing to do, not while the world is filled with so much misery, but I was struck by the encounter anyway.

I also know a dog called Anton. Because he's rather small, they also call him Antonchen. Antonchen. He's bold and cheerful, this Antonchen. He has a moustache.

And I know a dog called Jacques. He wears a fur coat with an astrakhan collar. He apparently once said he was cold, and ever since then he's walked around in this natty little outfit. Still, he does everything other dogs do, though I've never seen him laugh.

I don't dislike dogs. By and large, they're delightful creatures. Dogs have ears.

I have a dog myself. Or should I say that she has me? Whichever you prefer. She's been trotting beside me for more than ten years. Or me with her. Whichever. When I go into a shop, she waits outside. You go ahead, I'll wait here. I don't have to tie her up, that would be insulting. She waits, craning her neck to keep me in her sights, since it seems I once told her never to trust people completely.

She doesn't go to school, she hasn't ever been to school. And yet we've learned so much together that she never has to be put on a leash, not even in the busiest of streets. Me neither, by the way. And I don't need to shout at her, she doesn't think it's necessary. She barks only when the doorbell rings, and otherwise she's quiet. She burps occasionally. She has eyelashes and she snores. She slobbers when she drinks her water and spills a little onto the floor. And her tongue curls when she yawns.

The first time I took her into town with me, to the big, rough-and-tumble city, she spent the entire day coughing and hacking. A comment on air pollution, I suspect. She still does it if a car happens to roar off right next to her.

She'd never walk across my drawings, never. One time the doorbell rang. She barked, dashed towards the door and suddenly braked: there were three drawings on the floor. She does walk over newspapers, but not over drawings. She knows the difference between a newspaper and a work of art.

When I come home in the evening after roaming around the city, I find her waiting for me. She's getting on in years, so she no longer bounds to the door to greet me. Sometimes she's sound asleep, and the light makes her blink: Oh, is that you, how about going for a walk. We go. There's nothing more beautiful than the night in this wary neighbourhood.

She likes it when I'm gone in the evenings, I can tell. Why is that? What does she do when she's alone?

Does she read? I don't think so, but then how else do a couple of my books get moved? Does she sing dirty songs? Does she play records? Why is the phone bill so high? I can't ask her, she doesn't answer. And yet she's eleven years old.

What's been going on in my absence? Sometimes it seems as if she's been up to something she doesn't want me to know about, as if she's just slammed a book shut. She taps her fingers and whistles under her breath: nothing's the matter, I'm just a dog. Good. The wind whooshes through the room, the curtains billow: she's opened the window, she wanted some fresh air. Good.

Can dogs talk? Perhaps. I think they can, but don't want to. Because if they could, they'd also be able to go out and look for a job, and they're not about to do that. They want to be taken care of. Oh, they're willing to do a little something in return from time to time. Fetch or carry or show the way.

Once I went so far into the woods after midnight that I got lost, which doesn't happen very often, but it's a maze of trees with hundreds of dark corners. 'Go home,' I said to the dog, and she brought me home. She walked a few feet ahead of me, so that I could see her, and she kept turning around to make sure I was still there. She didn't run off to sniff the bushes, no, she was showing the way. She had a job to do, and she brought me to the door. I said a few words of thanks, and she did a little dance because we'd made it safely home, though she'd known all along that we would.

Oh, the kind-hearted Central European with his soft spot for animals. He knows that the majority of children are cruel, not kind, and that they tend to treat animals roughly. When that happens, he points out to the children in question that they ought to love all animals, except fleas and dung-flies. I recently spent a great deal of time in the countryside in Italy, where things are different.

The children of the farmer who lived in the next valley were real live wires. I believe such children are referred to as sweet little rascals, but they kicked the dog unmercifully, while the parents stood by nodding amiably, oh those kids.

And Mario, gentle, helpful, honest-as-they-come Mario (I mean this) saw a rabbit on the road. I was sitting beside him in the front seat, and he did his best to run it over. Not because he was a sadist, of course not. No, just because it was there. I suppose he pictured it in the roasting tray. He didn't manage to hit it, thank goodness, even though it was a bit on the fat side. He was sorry, I was relieved. It seemed like a nice rabbit.

It's different here. I'm sitting in a restaurant near the Kurfürstendamm, reading and waiting for my supper. The chefs are larking around in the kitchen and grinning. It's not very busy, so they aren't even wearing their hats. I take that back, they're just putting them on. A dog comes in, a yellow dog, and places his forepaws on the wooden partition between the kitchen and the dining room. The dog is asking if there's anything for him to eat. The chefs answer politely, telling him that he's too early, that he should come back in an hour or so. The dog seems a bit insulted. Without another word, he turns and leaves the dining room. I get up from the table to see where he's going.

Outside, a little old lady is waiting for him in Breitscheidplatz, next to the Gedächtniskirche. She can often be found near this church, because the Kaiser, the Kaiserin and her ladies-in-waiting once greeted her there. At any rate she seemed to think so, and nothing has happened to make her change her mind. She tells the story to whoever will listen, including me. She knelt down and bowed her head, so let's hope the Kaiser and his entourage noticed. She says they did. They saw her and acknowledged her greeting. How does she know that? She doesn't, she likes to think they did. They saw her. And acknowledged her greeting? And acknowledged her greeting.

Now she's walking arm in arm with the big yellow dog over the Kurfürstendamm. The dog can talk and laugh and think. That much is clear.

Fragments

WOMAN: During the war I was around seventeen or eighteen years old and I had a lot of girlfriends. Some of their fathers were ministers in the Confessional Church, which means they were anti-Nazis. The daughters were fun-loving and vivacious. We got along very well, and still do. I didn't have any brothers, but many of my girlfriends did, so when it was time for one of them to go to the Front, he'd ask me to escort him to the train. Come on – come and see me off, they'd say. Not that I had anything going with those boys. No, we were just friends. And after I'd taken them to the station, they'd say, come on, stay on the train, it'll be stopping at such-and-such a place. And I was glad to do it. Some of them came home on leave once or twice, but then that was it, they'd been killed. I took so many to the station, but I can't remember even one coming back alive. Let me think. No, not even one. Isn't that sad?

*

MAN: The air raids on Berlin were terrible, of course, but the worst part was just after they were over. Horrible, the city burning, entire streets on fire, entire neighbourhoods, houses burning or collapsing, a rain of ashes. It was a living hell. And then we had to try and rescue people. I was in a rescue team. Sometimes you couldn't get people out, and yet you heard them screaming and calling. It was awful. I don't actually want to think about it anymore, but I can't get it out of my mind. I'm old now, and sometimes when I'm walking through Berlin I go past those streets and I think: it was here, that's where I heard the screams. And now you see new houses and children playing.

*

MAN: So, you're from Holland, are you? There're a couple of Dutch people I'd like to talk to sometime, but I don't know who they are. It's like this. I was a simple working-class lad from the middle of Berlin. It took a lot of blood, sweat and tears, but I managed to put together a collection of gramophone records, really nice ones from Electrola. Opera records. And when I finally came back from the Front (I was twenty at the time), I found out that foreign workers from Holland had plundered our house, or rather the ruins of what had been our house. All my records were gone. They'd been in the basement, and had survived the bombings in one piece. Yes, I know you can't do anything about the fact that those Dutch people stole my records, but it still rankles.

*

MAN: Back when the windows of Jewish shops were being smashed in or painted with anti-Jewish slogans, the Nazis also did my place over. One morning I arrived at my shop, and there was a big star painted on it and a couple of those slogans. I set to work removing the paint, which wasn't all that easy, and I grabbed a sign with a slogan on it, which they'd put in front of the door, and took it inside. Immediately a couple of those goons came rushing in and screamed that I should take the sign back outside right that minute, but I held onto it for dear life. Then they threatened me so much that I had to let go. I was beside myself. You know what it was about? My name sounds a bit Jewish, but I'm not Jewish, even though I had dark hair and brown eyes. They dragged me outside, they were going to show me what they did to Jews who protested. They took me down to the local police station, but those policemen knew me, they were customers of mine, and they told them I wasn't Jewish. So I was allowed to go back to my shop. But I can still see those bitches (there's no other word to describe them) standing outside my shop and saying to those guys: Get him, he's a Jew. And those bitches, excuse me for using that word again, were the very same ones who were always at the front of the queue when I was giving something away, at Christmas or whatever. Always first for a freebie, but then sending those thugs down on my shop.

*

MAN: I had to join the Wehrmacht for the last two years of the war. I hated all that military nonsense and I hated the Nazis, but I admired the Americans and the English, I had from the very beginning. I could speak fairly good English, and I practiced on my own as often as I could. So the first thing I did, when the opportunity finally presented itself, was to seek contact with the conquerors. After all that time, I wanted to talk to them. Well, I was never so disappointed in my whole life. They'd been ordered not to fraternize with the Germans. It was a terrible blow. I was just a kid, and it really threw me. I'd admired them so much, and now they didn't even want to talk to me!

*

MAN: I was in the Waffen SS. You bet I was. Absolutely. Every once in a while, I used to go to a reunion. Lots of fun. Now I don't have the time. I used to see Dutch people there. Did you know Dutch people were also in the SS? Nice guys, but just like the other foreigners, they were, how shall I put it, obsessed with ideology. I was never interested in all that. To me the Waffen SS was an elite corps, and the rest was bullshit. We rarely talked about ideology, we had to fight. I never listened to that 'racial science' crap. I didn't have it easy at the front (I was wounded a couple of times), but I thought of it as one big adventure. If I was young, I'd do it again. I'm sure you think I'm a fool, but that's how I look at it. Life's treated me all right. I have a wonderful family and a business of my own, with employees who have been with me for nearly thirty years. Nobody wants to leave, we're one big family, and together we earn a good living. I know we Germans have a lot of crimes on our conscience, I know that. But I wouldn't have missed that period in my life for the world. I'd be lying if I told you anything else.

*

110

WOMAN: I hear people saying nowadays that the Nazis came from the middle class. That seems to be the latest trend. I simply can't understand that. If you ask me, it just isn't true. Maybe from the lower-middle class, but even then only certain members of it, namely the losers. In our circles, middle-class circles you might call them, people laughed at those lunatics in their idiotic Stormtrooper uniforms. My family and all our friends thought Hitler's idea of a *Volksgemeinschaft*, a national community, was absolutely ridiculous. To them, it meant reducing everyone to the lowest common denominator. They were fond of saying: The Nazis are no better than the Communists. They still thought that, and yet, later, my father joined the Nazi Party. I'll tell you why. It was because he wanted the Nazis to stop poking their noses into his business, to put an end to their distrust and constant harping on whether or not he was politically reliable. It gave him a bit more freedom. And believe me, a lot of people felt the same way. But they had a devil of a time after the war trying to convince the Americans of that. They all had to fill in one of those questionnaires. Everyone who was a member of the Nazi Party is still suspect. I consider that the height of insanity.

*

MAN: My father was a Social Democrat, but as a boy I was totally under Adolf's spell. Of course I was. All of us kids were! We looked up at him with tears in our eyes, and shouted *Heil* as hard as we could. I can still see us standing there. Adolf was my idol. We though he was so great because he'd got people back to work. He'd lifted us out of poverty. Of course we all knew what a concentration camp was, but somehow, when it came to the Jews, we didn't put two and two together. I still remember asking: Father, why do those people have to wear a yellow star on their coats. Oh, my father replied, they're Jews, they're being sent to form a colony in Madagascar. For the rest I never heard or read any more about it, and I didn't give it a second thought. You had your own worries. I was at the Front for two years; I'd enlisted in the army. My father thought I was out of my mind. Two years in a tank. At least in a tank you were out of the wind, so I didn't notice the cold in Russia as much as the others did. I only came back to Berlin in '48, and little by little we learned how Adolf had taken us for a ride.

The Little Things in Life

I sometimes watch people, because I happen to be one myself. Every once in a while, I observe them out of the corner of my eye. To see what they're like and what they're doing.

People – I often see them around me. I realize I'm one too when I watch them.

The reason I'm saying this is that I was concentrating all my efforts on painting trees, or something that resembled trees, when I suddenly had to leave on an unexpected trip. Just as I was busy giving those wretched trees, which have been bothering me my entire life, more light and air (even though they don't deserve it), just as I was giving them an air of innocence (even though I know better), I had to take off on another trip. I needed to take care of some business, since you can't just paint and write for a living, no matter how much you'd like to. You have to make arrangements and keep an eye on things.

To amuse myself, I decided to concentrate on the Little Things in Life during this period. I decided to concentrate on two of their darkest manifestations: surprise and annoyance.

I was able to get started right away. In broad daylight. At the check-in counter of the airport, the passengers were asked whether they wanted smoking or non-smoking. Non-smoking, said the man in front of me. And then proceeded to light a cigarette the minute he sat down. This was only the beginning of my surprise. My fellow human beings are full of good intentions.

But let's take another case. The concert hall. A number of people have brought along cough drops. They wait until the orchestra reaches a quiet part and then unwrap their lozenges. They crackle, they rustle, they rattle. Or they play like mad with their beads and chains. Or scrape their nails over their patent-leather bags. You feel like placing a stick of dynamite under their seats, but that would bring you to the realm of the *Big* Things in Life, and I've decided not to go into those today.

So the question is: should all that business in the concert hall be considered reprehensible behaviour, and if so, do you have to let it annoy you? If you're firm and made of strong stuff, if you're unflappable, you won't be annoyed. Unfortunately, I'm not always unflappable enough. I keep trying to be unflappable, but too much unflappability can drive your neighbours insane. So I do get exasperated from time to time. In other parts of the world people are busy bumping each other off, and here I am getting annoyed at crackling wrappers. I suspect this is the good life.

Anyway, I generally do manage to hear a few snatches of music in the concert hall. Though the last time I went, the man behind me had a definite respiratory problem. His windpipe must have been out of order, because he wheezed and spluttered so much I missed every note. All I heard was the noise behind me. But why should I be allowed to go to a concert and a man like that not be allowed? Still, I wanted to ask him to sit somewhere else the next time, but that also seemed highly reprehensible.

There are many forms of reprehensible behaviour which fall into the category of the Little Things in Life. To cite a few: standing around talking in a dining-room with your posterior beside a full plate. Or worse: bending over to, say, tighten your shoelace, so that your posterior is even more visible beside a full plate. I once saw someone who, in a flash of pure loathing, stuck a fork in that particular part of the anatomy, but that, too, was highly reprehensible.

To continue: being the first to step off a tram or bus and blocking the doorway while you stand there trying to decide where you want to go. Ditto at the bottom of an escalator. Or coming late to a cinema, picking a seat in the front row and taking forever to remove your coat, all the while blocking everyone's view of the screen with your hydrocephalic head. Extremely reprehensible. Talking loudly in hotel corridor early in the morning or late at night, behaving excitedly because you're in a foreign country, slamming the doors shut. Etc. etc.

Reprehensible behaviour. It does exist. Instead of thanking

your lucky stars that you're more or less in good health and are able to walk down the street without fear of persecution or arrest, you keep your eyes peeled until one of your fellow human beings does something that annoys you, even though you know it's going to make your blood pressure skyrocket. Aren't there more important things going on? Undoubtedly. But first of all, I suspect that big things begin as little things, and that the big things are reflected in the little things. Secondly, I promised to go into life's *little* things. So here goes.

On the Hohenzollerndamm, the bus driver was kind enough to wait for a little old lady who was sprinting towards the bus (she was still able to sprint). Nice of the driver. But once she was inside, he roared off so fast that she fell flat on her face. Even though she'd thanked him politely for waiting. Why he felt the need to get back at her is beyond me.

Our fellow human beings are incalculable and inescapable. I sometimes wonder what I've got involved in. Myself perhaps. But let's continue.

Not long after the war, I went to see the Black Forest. There had just been a big fire. A few years ago the mood hit me, and I went back. So I already knew that this forest had a large number of clearings. And that they were particularly mean at that spot. But I wanted to see the clearings anyway, as if I hadn't seen enough. I saw miles and miles of them and accomplished very little, which I might have known beforehand.

But there I was walking furiously though the Black Forest one day. I emerged from a pitch-dark wood, and suddenly a veil was lifted. It was light, there was a meadow. At the edge of that meadow was a horse. An ordinary horse with a mane and four legs. He'd gone over to the side to do a bit of thinking.

A few yards away was a sign, stating that there was a horse in this meadow and asking you please not to give him any food, especially not sugar cubes, because they weren't good for him, and besides, he got enough to eat, so please don't feed the horse. A man came walking up from the other side. Since he was looking at the horse, he didn't see me. He thought he was alone.

He put on his glasses and read the sign. I saw his lips moving. After he'd read the entire thing, he pulled a sugar cube out of his pocket and fed it to the horse. I nearly applauded at this excellent example of determination and sheer cussedness.

People are driven by dark-red desires. They can't help it, and yet it doesn't make them happy. They know precious little about these desires, but they think words will explain them. They use words to put up walls and protect themselves, and that takes up a goodly portion of their day. They weigh their words, eat them, mince them and put them in other people's mouths. They believe they've found a reasonable explanation.

I've read that the word 'man' is derived from the Sanskrit 'manas', which means 'mind'. So people are their minds.

I've heard it said, more than once, that people are creatures of reason. But if you take a closer look, you'll see that reason has usually subordinated itself to a more powerful force, that it's usually at the beck and call of something else. Who's really running the show is anybody's guess.

I don't have time for the Little Things in Life right now. I don't want to observe them. I need to go back to painting those trees. If I still can, that is. It'll be hard, but I'll manage. Just as we use words to explain our desires, I try to use paint to explain the trees. Though I could tell you a thing or two about those trees. Because the ones you see here are not to be trusted. Of course I'm referring to the *old* ones. Long may they live.

We Didn't Know Anything About It

I ought to say something about the children of the parents. About the generation that got a taste of the war, the generation that grew up, goodness knows how, into today's adults, whatever that means.

Their parents have been accused of not mourning. Well, the children have more than made up for it. They're noticeably good at mourning and groaning.

I warn you that I'm going to start generalizing, but I have to, in order to be clear.

So it's those children, now fully grown, who are constantly complaining to me that their parents never told them about their lives under National Socialism, about their attitude to *that time*. They never said a word.

Of course, that's probably true.

The parents probably kept their mouths shut for a variety of reasons. Because they were guilty as hell, because they'd been cowards, because they'd been zealots from the word go, or maybe also because they were genuinely ashamed, or stupid, or slow to catch on, or because they simply couldn't talk about it anymore, since they'd blocked it out or had been working somewhere else and had never got around to it. For the simple reason that they were people who ate their porridge in the morning and their potatoes at night. People with hand-brakes in their heads. Surely you don't think we haven't got them as well.

Oh, those parents who never said a word. Honesty compels me to say that I sometimes hear the opposite. In fact, I keep hearing it more and more often: My children never wanted to know a thing about it, they still don't, they're not in the least bit interested. It's a common refrain.

It also happens to be true. If you ask them about their parents, they appear to know surprisingly little. Yes, my father spent a few years in a POW camp, or at any rate I think he did. Allied or

117

Russian? Eh, I'm not sure. Which branch of the service was he in? Dunno.

They don't know a thing. Why is that? It's because they don't give a damn. And that, too, is a fairly normal reaction. After all, we didn't want to hear all those stories our parents told us about how hard their lives had been. How they had no opportunity to get an education but had had to go out and work for a living, while you're able to go to school and learn whatever you want. Not that I hated learning, mind you, I just hated school. I hated regimentation, and they found that hard to understand. So we've all failed to put ourselves in each other's shoes, but it was easier that way.

The children of those parents also complain that they didn't learn anything about Nazism in school.

There must have been many teachers in Germany back then who had their reasons for not talking about it. But what about Holland. I wasn't taught anything about Nazism either. Most schools didn't get any further than World War I. Of course, right after '45 little or nothing was said in my school about the war; we were all glad it was over. We had other things on our minds.

The same thing even happened under the Nazis. I realize this adds to the complexity, but the total picture can never be too complex. The writer Horst Krüger tells us that although he went to school at the Grunewald Gymnasium in Berlin, they never got any further than Bismarck. And that was under the Nazis.

I remember hearing people complain during the 1950s that children no longer knew who Anton Mussert was, and he'd been the leader of the Dutch National Socialist party. Most of the kids, it was said, didn't even know who Hitler was – one child thought he was a German cyclist. A wave of criticism swept over the teaching profession and quickly subsided. And we're not talking about Germany, but about Holland, which had been *occupied*. In case you didn't know.

I was recently reading a German newspaper and came across a guilt-ridden review that went something like this: Such and such a book has just been reprinted, an outstanding book on the Nazi concentration camps, first printed in 1961, but the fact that it has only just been reprinted is a shocking commentary on the mechanism of denial in Germany. According to the review.

No, it is not a comment on the mechanism of denial in Germany. I didn't see anyone in Holland rushing to reprint the book either, even though Holland had been, how could I ever forget it, *occupied* and therefore had good reason to point an accusing finger at the Germans. And yet, with a few exceptions, many outstanding books on the subject either sold poorly or not at all in Holland. Even in the '50s, the war seemed far away and long ago. Publishers and newspaper editors let it be known that they had little or no interest in the topic and that virtually no one was interested in the war anymore.

When the TV serial 'Holocaust' was shown here in Germany, the children of the parents really started squawking: I didn't know, it's an absolute disgrace, our parents and teachers didn't tell us, we didn't know anything.

They could have known, because hundreds of books and films about the war have appeared since '45. They simply didn't care. Which is their perfect right, except that then they shouldn't go around feeling sorry for themselves and grumbling about their own ignorance.

In this respect they're exactly like their parents, who have also continued to claim they didn't know anything about it.

Even so. Since when, I ask myself, does a young person *not* know something because his parents or teachers didn't tell him or her. How dare you bemoan the fact that you don't know something because your parents didn't tell you.

They may not realize it, but they too are saying '*wir haben es nicht gewusst*: we didn't know anything about it.' And it's not a lie. They could have known it, just like their parents. It.

Ah, but that's the catch: people aren't like that. They just aren't. You shouldn't expect too much of them.

They have so many other things to think about that their little grey cells get saturated, and they can't let anything else in. It's a question of self-preservation. The psychologist Manès Sperber calls this 'practical ignorance'.

I know people in Holland (yes, in Holland) who lived a stone's throw away from a concentration camp, but who could tell you almost nothing about it after the war. There was no point in making yourself more miserable, so they simply shut out whatever they could. Still, that doesn't necessarily make them lesser human beings. People like that sometimes offered, right when you least expected it, to help others.

Idealists think you can teach people everything. They believe in a land of milk and honey. I don't think people can be taught everything. What you can do is keep them under control. Through the Church, or through a political party that cracks the whip and makes sure that its followers do its bidding. But even then there are no guarantees.

As I recall, tram drivers in Amsterdam used to ask their passengers daily to move to the rear. (For all I know they still do.) Yet those who do shuffle towards the back, in other words those who bear the needs of others in mind, are an exception.

But perhaps that old battle-axe who won't move to the rear and thinks of no one but herself and wishes everyone outside the tram would drop dead is the very one who would offer to hide you in her home. You never know.

Fragments

MAN: Just imagine, I was lying there on the Russian front, in the mud, with another lad. We were barely eighteen years old. We lay flat on our stomachs for hours and hours in the silence. Our own men were a long way behind us, and we lay there in that huge lonely landscape all by ourselves. Still, we knew there was a sniper in the woods. Snipers lie in wait for you for hours until they get a chance to blow your brains out. It's a kind of game. Suddenly the bloke next to me says: Here, mate, got a cigarette? Yes, I'd saved one, my last one. We split it and we talked a little, and half an hour later he gets a bullet right in the head. Dead. I go through his pockets so I can take his personal effects back with me to the rear, and what do I find but a whole packet of cigarettes. And he'd asked me for my last cigarette. I've never been able to work that one out.

*

WOMAN: I was twenty when the war broke out. Whenever I think back to that period, I see myself waving goodbye at some station or another. Time and time again, standing by a train and waving goodbye.

*

MAN: I was seventeen when I volunteered for the army. Or maybe I should say for Hitler. I went through the entire offensive in the Ardennes. We were all dead keen. Propaganda was all we'd ever heard at school and at Hitler Youth meetings. We'd been indoctrinated with that nonsense for years. Yes, I really did believe in Hitler. I thought he was a kind of god. Until after the war, when I found out who and what I'd been fighting for. I was confused for a long, long time. Other blokes my age were able to shake it off, from one day to the next, but I never managed to. I never really got my bearings. So now I lead the antisocial life of a taxi driver who only drives at night. I've been at it for 25 years. I never go on holiday, since I have trouble switching from night to day. My body just can't take it anymore. I like the night. I'm a real night owl. I like the lights at night, and the sounds. For example, the sound of the rain pattering on the windows. I'm crazy about the night. You may not believe it, but as I drive I think about the past, about the time when I still had ideals. I was even married for a year, but my wife left me. She couldn't put up with my working hours, and I wasn't willing to give up the night for my wife. Nope. So I'm on my own, and I'm going to stay that way. It's how I'm happiest.

*

WOMAN: I'm half-Jewish, so you can understand why my family longed for the Russians to come liberate us here in Berlin. Well, I tell you, it was awful. As far as the Russians were concerned, there was no such thing as a good German. The only words they knew were *Frau* (woman) and *Uhr* (watch). Sometimes I thought, haven't you got enough watches? I can imagine not having enough women, but what can you do with all those watches. Sometimes their entire arms were lined with watches. I have a Jewish patient now who went into hiding when she was young, and of course she was happy when the Russians came. A truck full of soldiers drove past and she waved to them. They stopped. One of them yelled *Du Frau Hier* (You woman here) and grabbed her. Oh, you could say you were Jewish and had been in hiding, but a fat lot they cared. She was carted off to Russia along with other young women who'd been snatched off the streets, and she spent ten years (ten years!) in Russian camps. To this day she doesn't know why. She was suddenly released, and now she's moved back to Berlin. As you can imagine, she has a huge number of physical problems, but mentally she's in tiptop shape. People can be amazingly tough.

*

WOMAN: You must often have heard people say that the Russians really went berserk when they entered Berlin. It's true, it was a very bad time. Except that they were quite nice to us children. But don't forget: the Russians had nothing and the Americans had everything, so the Americans didn't need our possessions. The Russians hadn't been on leave in I don't know how long, and everything we had (and after the bombings, that wasn't much) was a luxury to them. Light from the roof and water from the wall, they said. By which they meant: a lamp on the ceiling and water from the tap. I'm not kidding. What did peasants from Kirghizia know about life in the city. They'd never been to Moscow or any other big city. They washed their clothes in the toilet bowl and did their business in the garden or even in the corner of the living-room. Later on another type of Russian arrived, and they were much more civilized. There were officers who spoke fluent German and had read German literature. But it was very bad in the beginning. My oldest sister's girlfriend was raped, and they beat her up so badly that she died a month later. What makes it even sadder is that she'd done a lot to help Jews in hiding. But let's drop the subject, it's pointless to think about it at this late date, absolutely pointless.

*

WOMAN: I was very much in favour of Hitler, because he got people working again. You can't imagine what a hard time we'd had, but then Hitler became Chancellor and things got better. You had the feeling you belonged again, you no longer felt like an outcast. Then he started the war, and I'll never forgive him for that. And to think he was the one who promised us peace. As for what happened to the Jews, well, that still bothers me. To ordinary people like us, the Jews were perfect examples of capitalist exploiters. And Hitler was opposed to capitalism, or at any rate, we thought he was. But then he should have made sure the guilty ones – and believe me, there were plenty of non-Jewish capitalists – were taken to court, instead of rounding up all the Jews, including the women and children, and having

123

them killed. He should never have done that. It was a terrible crime. A lot of Jews aren't capitalists at all. For example, they're good musicians. Did you know that?

*

WOMAN: My grandmother had seven children, and after the fourth one the Nazis gave you a *Mutterkreuz*, a kind of Iron Cross for mothers. They sent you a notice, and then presented the *Mutterkreuz* with a certain amount of ceremony. My grandmother didn't even bother to go get hers, and when they posted it to her she sent it back with a letter saying that she and her husband had wanted a large family, and had had the children for themselves and not for the Führer. I bet you think my grandmother was an anti-Nazi, but she wasn't. She didn't support the Nazis, but she didn't oppose them either. And it wouldn't have occurred to her to protest. I knew another woman like that. She had a Dachshund, and she hung her *Mutterkreuz* around its neck. The dog walked down the street wearing a *Mutterkreuz*. And that wasn't an act of protest either, though it could be interpreted as one. It just so happens that neither of the women got into any trouble over this. Oh yes, people like that did exist. But protest, no.

Eberhard

There's so much I don't understand that I feel it's worth bringing it up.

I don't understand the vast scheme of things: the coming and going of living creatures, the willpower of the planets, the movement of the clouds and the mouldering of the trees. I understand neither tempest nor twilight. That goes without saying. But neither do I understand the lever or the light switch. Nor the electric eel. I don't understand the landscape, I don't understand nature. Ah, nature. All right, spring was bound to come, it was nearly around the corner, and yet suddenly it snowed during the night. The next morning, the snow began to melt, so nature had gone to all that trouble for nothing. Nature has a mischievous streak. Or hasn't it. I tell you, nature is a tough nut to crack. But that's the point, I think.

I don't understand the woman who puts out bread for the birds in the woods beside my house every morning. It gets eaten by the dogs who are out on their walks. The birds can only sit and watch while the dogs eat their food.

Look, there's one munching away right this minute. I can hear its owner up ahead blowing a whistle. The dog burps and goes on eating. He lets her whistle, he hasn't finished. I know his owner: she never goes anywhere without that whistle hanging around her neck. I know the dog too. He's called Eberhard. That's his name: Eberhard.

Eberhard eats the bread because he's an animal, and animals don't give a hoot about their fellow creatures. When Eberhard's finished, he runs to catch up with his owner: Where on earth have you been? Eberhard's not about to tell her what he was up to. He pulls the wool over her eyes, says he had to move a stick, or something. They continue their walk.

But the woman who puts out the bread, doesn't she know that it gets eaten by the dogs and not by the birds? Yes, she does know, but she hopes she can talk them out of it. She tells them not to do it, says it isn't very nice of them, and then scatters more bread and calls the birds. Nearby, a blackish dog is lurking behind a tree. I can see his long ears. He's waiting for her to hurry up and go so he can eat the bread. I know this dog too. He's called Johannes. Johannes.

The bread lady is quite old. She has a broad face with high cheekbones and deep-set eyes. I like to look at faces like hers. You run into a lot of them in this region. I often see her talking to a dog who's just eaten the bread, admonishing it. She leans forward a little, so that her words will sink in better. The dog listens patiently and licks its chops. I see her pointing towards the sky, since that's where the birds fly.

The woman appeals to the dog's common sense. It's wasted effort, because dogs don't have common sense, they have dog sense, which is why they wolf down the bread. I think that's pretty much how it goes.

Oh, there's so much I don't understand. Until recently, a mother and son lived downstairs from me. From the age of twelve to the age of fifteen, the boy lived next to and across from the woods, but he never once set foot in them. I don't understand that. (Oh, how grim the woods were then, how determined the armies that prowled through them.)

He was a nice boy, but if he'd been my son I'd have given him a swift kick in the rear and said: Get a move on, go and talk to the animals and the trees, let a scintillating caterpillar tell you about life as a larva, rescue the first enchanted princess you meet from a slow, lingering death, slay dragons or give them a wide berth, whichever suits your fancy, and keep yourself from falling into the clutches of a knight-errant or try to become one yourself. But I've heard that you shouldn't kick sons.

I know someone else who lives on the edge of a wood, in another part of Berlin. A sculptor. He has his studio there. Trees rustle, birds chirp. But from early in the morning to late at night, he has his radio on full-blast. He hasn't even chosen the music himself, that's been done for him by people somewhere in a room they call a *studio*. The noise bounces off the high walls. That's his business, it has nothing to do with me. And yet I've heard him tell others that it's so nice and quiet in his studio. A hellish din all day long, and he was blatting on about 'quiet'. He also said that he voted for the Greens, because, he added, they want to protect the environment. He hasn't set foot in the woods either. That's not necessarily bad. Here they call a person like that a *Stadtpflanze*, a city plant. You're either a city plant or you're not, there's nothing you can do about it. I'm probably one too, but my buds and branches are of another, more debatable, make.

I don't understand the gyrations of my fellow human beings. I mean, I do understand them, but then again, I don't. I trust I've made myself perfectly clear.

Besides, this week I also caught a glimpse of the firmament. I tell you, I couldn't make head or tail or it. The firmament was feeling on top of the world, but had thrown all caution to the winds.

There's much more. Just for fun, let me tell you what one of them is called: two people approach one another. They suddenly grab each other's hands, move them up and down, bare their teeth, move their hands up and down again and then continue on their way. Of all things. At home, they say they ran into so and so. It seems that the business with the hands was a *meeting*.

I also once saw a man take off his hat. He was showing the other person his hair or something. I've even seen people touch each other with their lips. I'm pretty sure I've done it myself. After all, I also meet people. Certainly I do.

And yet I don't understand it. Who gives the order? Who told me how to walk? I walked. I'm still walking. I'm still on my feet. That's amazing.

People-Talk

One day I was walking through the city, on the pavement, amid the other pedestrians. I was wearing ordinary clothes. Not a costume, not the uniform of a bellboy or a Horse Guard or some such thing. No, I was inconspicuous. Though I probably was charged with electricity.

Suddenly a man grabbed me by the arm. He reeked of alcohol and was swaying on his feet. Hey, guv'ner, he said, get a load of that. Behind you. Have you seen that?

I looked behind me and saw a huge, purple, cloud-flecked sunset. The sun was taking its leave that day with a hearty laugh.

Isn't it just great? he asked.

Yes, it was. He'd seen it with his yellowy eyes. I hadn't, I hadn't seen it.

I was stopped another time in that same spot by a man with a bottle in his hand.

– Hey, you there, is it Monday today?

– No, it's Sunday.

– Oh, *Scheisse*.

Actually, I was on my way to visit the man who was about to tell me he'd been a *Schlappier* his entire life. That's a word they use in Berlin, pronouncing it the French way. We'd call him a wimp.

Before and during the war, he had a secretary. She was a capable woman, but extremely unattractive. Or at any rate he thought so, because she had a rumpled mouth and square legs. She soon found out when his birthday was, and every year she gave him something for the office. A rug, an inkwell, a letter-opener, a pencil-sharpener, a picture frame, a blotting pad, a pencil-box. It depressed him. His desk was covered with things he didn't like.

She kept a sharp eye on him. One time he took a particularly ugly and useless object home. The next day she asked him if he hadn't like it. Oh, that wasn't it, he'd said, he liked it a lot, and he'd brought the thing straight back to the office.

What could he do. He couldn't fire her, she was far too good a secretary. Besides, if he suggested it, she'd advise him against it, in all seriousness.

Business was going well, but when it came to her, he had absolutely no say in things. He hardly dared to talk to her. He was relieved when his call-up papers came and he was sent to the Front.

There, in the heart of Russia, he received a letter from his secretary, telling him that his office no longer existed, that it'd been bombed into oblivion.

He wasn't sorry. He was glad that the desk with the ugly objects wasn't there anymore.

But why had he let himself be browbeaten by his secretary. Because, as he himself says, he's a *Schlappier*.

The same gutless wonder also recounted a story from much longer ago, when he was still a boy. One time he and his brothers were allowed to dine with his parents and his aunts and uncles. They ate a leisurely meal, while the servants raced to and fro. Dessert was a long time in coming, so the children were given permission to step down, as long as they didn't make any noise. He and his brothers ducked underneath the broad table and tried to guess which legs belonged to which aunt.

'One of my aunts,' he said, 'must have thought, "Oh, the boys are growing up, so let's really give them something to look at." And she did. We could hardly believe our eyes.' Deeply impressed, they came out from under the table, silently ate their desserts and were quiet for a long time afterwards. Every once in a while, they glanced at the aunt, but she was busy talking.

Stories. Memories. Other people's words.

I sometimes try to *stroll* through the city. It isn't easy. I'm always on the run. I'm impatient, afraid I might miss something.

I'm in such a hurry, I miss everything. Every once in a while, contrary to all expectations, I do manage to stroll. In hopes of catching a few snatches of people-talk.

Like the man who says he ships timber to Poland to have cupboards and tables made, and then hauls them back to Berlin so he can sell them at a cheaper price than the cupboards and tables manufactured in Berlin.

Or the lawyer who had an appointment that morning with a woman who wanted to gripe about her marriage. She'd been married to the same man for over thirty years, and she spoke of him with great bitterness. But haven't you ever thought of a divorce? the lawyer asked. No, said the woman, but I have thought of murder.

Or the tall, grey-haired woman who tells me that when her husband (he'd been her fiancé at the time) was a soldier in Russia, he went to see a fortune-teller, who predicted that he'd die before he was forty. To his surprise, he wasn't killed in action. He was in a POW camp for a couple of years, but he survived that too. He came back, they got married, they built up a business and life was treating them fine. But her husband apparently never forgot the Russian fortune-teller, because on the day before his fortieth birthday he committed suicide. Hung himself.

From time to time I have a more charming encounter: an elderly couple, both in their eighties, still in good health. They enjoy being together. They both play the violin – some very nice pieces have been composed for two violins. Or as they put it: We'll keep on playing till we die.

Fragments

WOMAN: Right after the war, most of the kids in my class had lost their fathers, while my father came back. Well, they never let me forget it. They practically blamed me because my father wasn't dead. You only really counted to the other kids if your father had been killed. A father who was missing in action was okay, but not as good, since he might still turn up. But if he'd simply come home, they said: Oh, but your father didn't really fight. Or they accused him of having been a coward or a shirker.

*

MAN: I was an odd kind of soldier. I never fired a single shot. I was ill the whole time, and I was transferred from one hospital to the next because I was covered with a rash, with eczema. Oh, the suffering I saw in the hospitals. It is indescribable. And there I lay, a young boy, not harmed in the least, except that I was covered with salve from head to toe, while all around me were blokes my age who'd lost an arm or a leg or even worse. Everywhere I looked there were the wounded and the dying. The minute the war was over, my symptoms disappeared. Haven't had a bit of trouble since.

*

MAN: I was in the Waffen SS and not even twenty when the war ended. Huh. You know what I said when I heard that Hitler was dead? I said that it was our fault, that we Germans weren't good enough for our Führer. A lot of people were saying that, I wasn't the only one. That's how much of a true believer I was. I say *true believer*, because I absolutely worshipped that man. And now? Oh, I think that after the war we were well on our way to a strong democracy, but I'm afraid that the present generation is ripe for a new dictatorship. It's clear in everything they do and say that most young people don't give a damn about anything having to do with democracy. They're just as foolish as we were in our day. Except for one thing: they ought to know better.

*

MAN: You know what really gets my goat? That there are always new people, young people, who think they know better, who think they can do it better. Every time it happens I'm surprised – and annoyed. The first time I ran into one of those types was on the Russian front. We were experienced soldiers, seasoned veterans. We knew everything we needed to, and in walks some young officer, fresh from the Academy, and he was sure he knew better. We had to do it his way. During the next attack I said: I'm not gonna do it, nope, not me. But I had no choice. Well, everything went wrong. We got in each other's way, people panicked, and my best friend was killed about ten yards ahead of me. I couldn't get to him. I wanted to retrieve his papers, but I couldn't get to him, and that still bothers me. I just couldn't get to him. That damned officer, who thought he knew better. I still remember his name. I'm never going to forget him, not as long as I live. See, that's what I mean. All those young whippersnappers who are sure they know how things should be done. You can see it happening all over again. They can hardly wait to tell us how it should be done. Just who do they think they are? I can't stand people like that.

*

WOMAN: I went to a girls' school here in Berlin. We never talked about politics. Try as I might, I can't even remember whether any of the teachers were Nazis. No, I don't have the faintest recollection. Nor whether anyone ever said Heil Hitler. I don't think we did. I do know that a soldier came to the school once, to inform us of something, I suppose. He was what was known as a *Schwarzer*: a man in the black uniform of the SS. But he wasn't even given a cup of tea. We didn't like the SS. Someone from the Wehrmacht got a cup of tea, but a Schwarzer, no.

MAN: At the end of the war I was a nineteen-year-old officer. Now that's what you call a *young* officer. I may have been young, but I was also very old, if you know what I mean. I wound up in an American POW camp, somewhere in Bavaria. One day they put together a transport of young officers who came from Berlin and had been given permission to go home. Of course that meant passing through the Russian zone. We were happy as hell – we'd been in that camp for almost a year. (This was late in 1946.) But I was an awkward cuss, and for some reason I felt uneasy. So just before we reached the Russian zone, I decided to do a bunk, though nobody else wanted to go with me. It took me a year to get to Berlin because I had to follow a pretty roundabout route, but that's another story. Of course I was sorry I'd legged it. But after I got back to Berlin I heard that none of the men in that transport had made it home. The Russians had killed them all. I tell you, hearing that really gives you a funny turn. I still haven't worked out why the Russians would go and do a thing like that.

*

MAN: During the war I had a big chemist's shop in Berlin, and after one of those heavy bombing raids, after one of those awful nights, I went to my shop in Wilmersdorf. Well, it wasn't there anymore, it'd been completely wiped out. I remember saying to my next-door neighbour: Well, it's not a total disaster, I recently bought a smaller chemist's in another part of town, so I'll just carry on with that one. So I went there, but it was gone too. Besides that, I had a warehouse in another district. Also gone. I lost everything I owned in one night. There was nothing left. To add insult to injury, I got my call-up papers on the same day. So I reported to the recruitment office. I got one of those real old-fashioned officers with a monocle. I complained that the call-up papers had come at an unfortunate time, since I'd lost all my businesses and needed to take care of matters. Well, he said, that's good timing, because as long as you've lost everything you might as well be sent to the Front. I was so furious my ulcer started bleeding right then and there – I'd been having quite a bit of trouble with ulcers. So I didn't go into the service. And my ulcer never played up again either.

The Sun

Since I never wear spats, can do without a hat and walking-stick and don't need an overcoat, I can simply open my front door and step outside. And when I do, I find myself in the heart of Berlin. How did that happen?

Well, I'm no longer living on the outskirts of the woods, I'm no longer living in the studio of the controversial painter. I miss the smell of the trees. I miss their pluckiness. I miss the stories they tell me as well as the ones they don't.

And I miss the dog. She's dead.

Just before she died, she asked me to say hello to everyone who'd ever petted her or talked to her and to wish them well. She also said it wouldn't be right for me to mourn her a long time, since she was just a dog. I didn't always agree with her, but I have to admit that she was very wise. She was a living being, capable of moving around and having feelings. She could carry sticks, read maps, do arithmetic, sing, and a whole lot more. Besides that, she was neat and tidy, a neat and tidy dog.

I wonder where she is now. Is she really gone, or is she somewhere near? Perhaps she's been reincarnated into another animal. Into, say, a mosquito or another dog. Or a human being with high moral standards. I think it's better not to ask things that are none of your business. They're meant to be secrets.

There are so many secrets. People scatter words to the winds, and occasionally somebody comes along and picks them up. But secrets stay right where they are. If you ask me, the number of secrets keeps growing daily, and it's just as well.

So now I'm living in a street filled with memories and footsteps, a street full of past grandeur. A few doors down is the former residence of Hedwig Courths-Mahler. She lived there for eighteen years, between 1914 and 1932. It's also where she wrote her imaginative novels: in a house on the corner overlooking Goethestrasse. Of all places. She didn't write on Fridays, because

135

that's when she received the celebrities of her day: Asta Nielsen, Emil Jannings, Richard Tauber, Franz Lehar. All of whom must have passed down my street.

If I go the other way, I come to the Savignyplatz. After the war, George Grosz lived in number 5. He came back from exile in America and ended up at that address because that's where his mother-in-law lived.

Why did some people return to Germany while others didn't? One had no desire to ever set foot in that hated country again, while another couldn't wait to go back to the land that had driven him or her out. So where did they live? Cities like Berlin were in ruins, and at first they were almost uninhabitable. Yes, it's strange, but people like that are strange.

George Grosz whiled away many a night in a bar called Diener's, in nearby Grolmanstrasse. It's still there. In 1959 a newspaper boy found him on his front porch, and a few hours later he was dead. That was the end of George Grosz.

Things like that happen in this neighbourhood. And much, much more, though I don't know everything and I hope I never will, because it can trigger all kinds of thoughts.

Thanks to the drawings Grosz made before and after World War I, we think we know what capitalists looked like, though of course they didn't really. His friend Kurt Tucholsky put it this way: 'But German bankers don't look that greedy, that fat, that big . . . they collect porcelain, they usually have smaller heads . . . they look different . . . not better, just different.' Grosz stretched the truth and blew it out of proportion, because he was an artist, and moreover, one filled with hate. But his drawings were magnificent, and in my opinion, that's what it's all about.

It can't do any harm to have a look at the diaries of Harry Graf Kessler. This fanatical *Zeitbeobachter*, observer of his contemporaries, knew almost everybody in Berlin. Naturally that included Grosz, some of whose works he bought. In an entry written in 1919 he called Grosz a 'cultural Bolshevik', and reported a conversation with him, in which Grosz said that art is unnatural, a disease, and that the world doesn't need art, that people can also live without art. Grosz was annoyed at the uselessness of art. He believed that art had to have a purpose again, like religious painting did centuries ago. Kessler noted: 'Both reactionary and revolutionary, a sign of the times.' And he added one last comment: '. . . besides that, his thoughts are intellectually primitive, and you can easily punch holes in his arguments.'

Grosz later agreed with him. He came to view everything he thought and did in his younger years as a lot of nonsense. But at the time he believed that the ruling class should be fought by every available means. Kessler argued that any ideal that had to be achieved by violence defeated its own purpose. Conversations that took place soon after World War I, and they're still going on.

So now you've been told a few facts about a painter and caricaturist, because I happen to live in the neighbourhood where he died.

Sure enough, there are trees in this street. My flat is located just above them. If I want, I can look down at their leafy crowns, but I never gaze at them for long, because the trees don't like it. They prefer you to look *up* to them.

Above the tree tops, I can see the sky. Fortunately, there are a few real clouds for a change, not that impenetrable fog.

To be honest, I don't like it much when the weather's *nice*. I have trouble working. I need clouds, thick, fast-moving clouds. Only then am I industrious and full of energy. During nice weather, I have to force myself to get down to business, and even then, I plod along with little result, which is quite tedious.

Besides, I harbour the suspicion that there's no such thing as 'nice' weather anymore.

Things were different before the war. The streets were dotted with horse manure. And the sun was different. It was round and yellow. It shone. I tried to catch a glimpse of it sometimes, but it didn't let me. It simply shone. Look, people said, the sun is shining.

Now somebody, I don't know who, has placed a big warm

hood over our heads, and we call it the sun. It doesn't give off warmth the way it used to or the way it still does in more southerly climes. No, it's an oppressive kind of heat. I never have headaches, so I shouldn't be the one to talk, but on days like that many people clutch their heads and moan about the heat. Here they say it's *schwül*: sultry.

No, wait a minute, that's not true, I've made a mistake. I've just been informed that the sun that was there before the war is the same one that was there after the war. Ten minutes ago a young salesgirl told me that she had clear memories of the sun when she was a child. During school trips she'd been so happy to see what she called the 'golden' sun. Back in those days there used to be a real sun. But it's gone now, she added, and she's never seen it again. So that's that.